Aligarh
Muslim
University

Aligarh Muslim University

THE MAKING OF
THE MODERN INDIAN MUSLIM

MOHAMMED WAJIHUDDIN

HarperCollins *Publishers* India

First published in India by
HarperCollins *Publishers* 2021
A-75, Sector 57, Noida, Uttar Pradesh 201301, India
www.harpercollins.co.in

2 4 6 8 10 9 7 5 3 1

P-ISBN: 978-93-5489-331-5
E-ISBN: 978-93-5489-332-2

Cover design: Saurav Das
Cover Image: Getty Images

Typeset in 11.5/15.7 Warnock Pro at
Manipal Technologies Limited, Manipal

Printed and bound at
Thomson Press (India) Ltd

❶❿◉⊙HarperCollinsIn

To Abba and Ammi, who would have felt proud today

Contents

Introduction

NOTED Urdu satirist and humourist Rasheed Ahmad Siddiqui (1892–1977) had a delightful pastime. Whenever he came across a well-mannered stranger, he would ask him whether he had ever been a student at Aligarh Muslim University (AMU). It would please Siddiqui if the stranger turned out to be an AMU alumnus; it didn't surprise him at all that the stranger was so charming. But it saddened Siddiqui if the refined stranger told him that he had never studied at AMU. Siddiqui would feel sorry that such a nice person had been deprived of the nemat or boon of studying at AMU.

If Siddiqui were to return to the AMU campus today, he would be hugely disappointed. The 'Aligarh ethos' that had moulded him and countless others, and which he longed to discover was behind any decent denizens he would meet, is gone. Yes, there are well-cut black sherwanis and tight-fitting churidar-pyjamas aplenty on display, especially on ceremonial occasions like the founder Sir Syed Ahmad Khan's (1817–1898) birthday on 17 October, which is celebrated as 'Sir Syed Day' by Aligs, or alumni of AMU, globally. A sherwani, churidar-pyjama and Turkish cap for men, and niqab or a hijab for women, were once the uniforms on the campus. M. Hashim Kidwai (1921–2017), who taught political science at AMU and served the university as provost of the residential halls and proctor of the university before he became a Rajya Sabha member (1984–1990), writes in his autobiography, *The Life and Times of a Nationalist Muslim,* that the sherwani and the Aligarh-cut pyjama began taking a backseat in the late 1950s. Until then, the male students wore sherwani and churidar even during summers. Things changed after the introduction of the bush shirt, and in the summer months the old uniform was discarded. Now, a minuscule minority dons the uniform that used to be the distinctive feature of the campus.

The dress code at AMU had entered the popular imagination, so much so that Hindi cinema had lapped it up. Remember the debonair Rajendra Kumar, smartly dressed in a white sherwani-churidar, crooning the romantic number '*Mere mehboob tujhe meri mohabbat ki kasam, mera khoya hua rangeen nazara dede*' (My beloved, please return my lost romantic view) from the 1963 film *Mere Mehboob*? The song features a scene where a sherwani-clad Rajendra Kumar unintentionally collides with the burqa-clad Sadhana, clutching a bunch of books to her chest. The books fall and both kneel down to pick them up. While doing so Kumar touches Sadhana's hands, a reason for the poet Shakeel Badayuni to describe the scene in the sugary, romantic strain '*Marmari haathon ko chchua tha maine*' (I had touched those marble-like hands).

That popular image of AMU boys and girls is fading. And the change is not merely sartorial. It is also in the way AMU is perceived. For decades in the last century, AMU remained an epicentre of Muslim politics, a nerve centre of Indian Muslims' intellectual life. It made or marred the 'Muslim destiny' like no other institution.

However, despite the noticeably painful downfall in the delightful tradition and culture Aligarh (the city of Aligarh and AMU became interchangeable over time) used to boast of, AMU does retain some of its original charms. *Mara hathi bhi sawa lakh ka hota hai* (even a dead elephant fetches Rs 1.25 lakh), goes a popular Hindi idiom, denoting the value of a once-giant entity. Despite its considerably reduced utilitarian value for the community—after all, one university cannot fulfil the educational needs of a twenty-crore-strong community in the country—AMU remains a centre of intellectual life for Indian Muslims. As Akhtarul Wasey, professor emeritus at Jamia Millia Islamia (JMI), Delhi, and president of Maulana Azad University, Jodhpur, puts it: 'It is the largest hub of intellectuals in the Muslim world. Nowhere in the world you will find so many educated Muslim minds concentrated at one place.' Dr Zakir Hussain (1897–1969), AMU alumnus, its former vice chancellor (VC) (1948–1956) and later President of India, summed up AMU's roadmap thus: 'The way Aligarh participates in various walks of national life will determine the place of Muslims in Indian national life. The way India conducts itself towards Aligarh will largely, yes, will largely, determine the form that our national life will acquire in the future.'[1]

It is against this backdrop that Prime Minister Narendra Modi's virtual address to the AMU at its centenary celebrations on 22 December 2020 commanded importance. (The

Madrasatul Uloom Musalmanan-e-Hind, founded in 1875 by Sir Syed Ahmad Khan, graduated to the Muhammadan Anglo-Oriental [MAO] College in 1877, further metamorphosing into AMU in 1920.) It has been a remarkable journey of a century since the Aligarh Muslim University Act was passed on 1 December 1920 and the university's inauguration on 17 December 1920. In that memorable televised speech, Modi killed two birds with one stone. He silenced, albeit temporarily, the section in the Sangh Parivar that has always viewed AMU with suspicion and seen it as a bastion of 'Muslim separatism' and an incubator of 'fifth columnists'. However short-lived people think it may be, Modi's assurance to the AMU community and its vast circle of sympathizers was that the ruling dispensation in India has stopped seeing AMU with a jaundiced eye. He left nothing to the imagination when, in his characteristically convincing style, he declared: 'We see a mini-India [at AMU] among different departments, dozens of hostels, thousands of teachers and professors. The diversity which we see here is not only the strength of this university but also of the entire nation. [The] History of education attached to AMU buildings is India's valuable heritage.'[2]

In May 2018, AMU was rocked by a controversy over a portrait of Pakistan founder Mohammad Ali Jinnah that had been hanging in the AMU Students' Union Hall since 1938. The Bharatiya Janata Party's Aligarh Member of Parliament Satish Gautam sent a letter to AMU Vice Chancellor Dr Tariq Mansoor demanding the removal of Jinnah's portrait from the campus. Just a few days earlier, some students had asked for an RSS shakha to be set up at the AMU campus. On 2 May 2018, around two dozen youths affiliated to right-wing outfits stormed the varsity, protesting against the Jinnah portrait.

Several students were injured when they clashed with police outside the university's main gate, Bab-e-Syed. Student leaders alleged that the right-wing activists wanted to hurt former vice president, former VC and AMU alumnus M. Hamid Ansari, who was on the campus at the time for a programme. Ansari was scheduled to be awarded the students union's honorary life membership, an honour the students had bestowed on Jinnah in 1938. Jinnah's portrait has been hanging on the union hall's wall since then. But the first person to decorate this wall of fame had been Mahatma Gandhi. The AMU boys had felicitated him in 1920, eighteen years before Jinnah got the same honour.

On 30 May 1939, Jinnah wrote his will, according to which all his properties were to be divided into three parts. One part was to be bequeathed to AMU, one part to Islamic College, Peshawar, and one part to Sindh Madrassa, Karachi. 'Through this will, Aligarh Muslim University will be within its rights to demand its share in the Jinnah House in Mumbai. But AMU never did. There are many unkind, unpleasant things in history and tradition. Do we go on demolishing all these unpleasant things? That portrait is also part of a tradition,' argues Shafey Kidwani, senior professor of mass communications at AMU.

Jinnah, who visited AMU many times, had once described it as 'the arsenal of Muslim India.'[3] He first visited AMU in 1925, when it celebrated the golden jubilee of the founding of the school. Subsequently Jinnah visited the university several times, especially between 1938 and 1944, garnering support from the youthful, energetic band of boys there for the Muslim League.

On 23 March 1940, the All-India Muslim League passed a resolution in Lahore seeking autonomy for the Muslim-majority states of Punjab, Bengal, Sindh and the North West Frontier Province of British India. Many saw it as a demand for a separate Muslim nation, state, calling it the Pakistan Resolution. The resolution was presented at Minto Pak in Lahore. This park was later rechristened Iqbal Park, as a tribute to the poet-philosopher Allama Sir Mohammad Iqbal (1877–1938).

Why did they rename Minto Park as Iqbal Park? There is a link between the March 1940 resolution and Allama Iqbal's presidential speech at the All-India Muslim League's annual session at Allahabad on 29 December 1930. The supporters of the two-nation theory could not have found a better person than Allama Iqbal for validation of what they had been demanding. In that speech Iqbal had said:

> I would like to see the Punjab, North West Frontier Province, Sind and Baluchistan amalgamated into a single State. Self-government within the British Empire, or without the British Empire, the formation of a consolidated northwest Indian Muslim State appears to me to be the final destiny of the Muslims, at least of northwest India.[4]

'Strangely Iqbal left out Bengal, which had a huge Muslim population, in his proposed "Muslim state", wrote scholar and politician Dr Rafiq Zakaria in his book *Iqbal: Poet and Politician*. He describes the scene at the Allahabad session of the Muslim League where Iqbal uttered these lines, which became a beacon for the proponents of Pakistan. Zakaria says that this was a tragic event. Initially the programme was planned at an open venue but had to be taken inside a zamindar's haveli, as a motley crowd of not more than 200 had turned up for the meeting. Hardly twenty or so delegates from outside had participated in this session. Allama Iqbal spoke in English, so the programme was boring for most of the attendees who couldn't understand the language. Maulana Amjad Ali Khan, editor of the famous Urdu magazine *Humayun*, carried a detailed report in the publication on the function. 'The Maulana reports that when Iqbal was reading out his speech in English, one Barrister-at-Law sitting beside him told him, "I don't understand what he is saying. I think he is speaking in Greek".[5]

Most of the audience had come there to hear Iqbal's poetry, not his boring speech, and they wanted Iqbal to recite some couplets. Iqbal got angry, but relented after the organizers intervened. At their request he recited a few couplets.

The communal historians unjustifiably credited Iqbal with having fathered the idea of Pakistan. Needless to add, there were many at AMU who liked Iqbal for having 'sided' with the demand for Pakistan. But the fact is that the Pakistan Resolution was passed in 1940, a complete ten years after Iqbal's Allahabad speech and two years after his death in 1938.

A great admirer of Sir Syed, Iqbal saw him as the renaissance man and paid glowing tributes to the old man of Aligarh through his poems. Iqbal's two poems—'*Syed ki Lauh-E-Turbat*' (Gravestone of Syed) and '*Talba-e-Aligarh College ke Naam*' (Dedicated to the Students of Aligarh College)—exemplify his deep love for and devotion to Sir Syed and his Aligarh Movement. Former AMU Vice Chancellor Mehmoodur Rahman, an ardent lover of Iqbal's poetry, got the last couplet of '*Syed ki Lauh-E-Turbat*' inscribed on the Bab-e-Syed. The couplet goes: '*Sonewalon ko jaga de sheir ke eijaz se/ Khirman-e-Batil jala de Shola-e-Awaz se* (Awaken the slumbrous with your eye-opening poetry/Burn the harvest of falsehood with the flame of your voice).'[6]

Undeniably, Aligarh did provide ammunition to the Muslim League's diabolic two-nation theory. However, as scholar and former vice chancellor of Jamia Millia Islamia Mushirul Hasan explains in his introduction to David Lelyveld's seminal work *Aligarh's First Generation,* Aligarh's 'second generation', represented by the likes of Mohammed Habib, Hamza Alavi, Rashid Ahmed Siddiqui, Zakir Hussain and a number of other poets and writers, '... repudiated the polemical two-nation theory and opposed the clamour for a separate nation'. For every Sahibzada Liaquat Ali Khan who studied at AMU and became the first prime minister of Pakistan, there was a 'Frontier Gandhi' Khan Abdul Ghaffar Khan, AMU alumnus and freedom fighter, who never reconciled to the vivisection of India.

M. Hashim Kidwai has mentioned a long list of MAO College students who participated in national politics. He writes:

A galaxy of national leaders, like the Ali Brothers (Muhammad Ali and Shaukat Ali), Dr Saifuddin Kitchlu, A.M. Khwaja, Dr Syed Mahmud, Rafi Ahmad Kidwai, Hasrat Mohani, Khan Abdul Ghaffar Khan, T.A.K Sherwani, Zafar Ali Khan, Raja Mahendra Pratap Singh, Dr Syed Husain, Chaudhary Khaliq-uz-Zaman, Yasin Nuri and Hafiz Mohammad Ibrahim were all products of the MAO College.[7]

Muhammad Ali also distinguished himself as a fiery speaker and a powerful commentator. His two newspapers—*The Comrade* in English and *Hamdard* in Urdu—unsettled the British Raj. His English was better than his Urdu. *The Comrade* became so popular that even European officials subscribed to it: 'Lady

Hardinge, the wife of the Viceroy, would phone if an issue was delayed.[8] The British government invited Muhammad Ali to participate in the 1930 Round Table Conference in London. For the first time, his wife accompanied to him to London and, for her trip, he had to borrow Rs 3,000 or Rs 4,000 from a friend. Addressing the British on 19 November 1930, Muhammad Ali had famously said: 'I would prefer to die in a foreign country so long as it is a free country, and if you do not give us freedom in India you will have to give me a grave here.'[9] He died on 4 January 1931 in England. His friends and family members buried him neither in Britain nor in India. He was buried near Bait-ul-Muqdas, the Dome of the Rock, in Jerusalem. Muslims believe that the Prophet ascended to the heavens from there. Muhammad Ali's elder brother Shaukat Ali, who had sheltered Muhammad Ali at MAO College and had stayed back in India to serve the British so that Muhammad Ali could study at Oxford, was among the pallbearers for his younger brother.

Another famous alumnus of MAO College who had an exhilarating journey was Syed Fazlul Hasan (1875–1951), who adopted the nom de plume of Hasrat Mohani. Hasrat did his BA from MAO College in 1903, ' ... but abandoned his further studies in law that he had joined soon after his graduation.'[10] A poet-critic and leader who coined the slogan '*Inquilab zindabad*' (Long live the revolution), Hasrat had the distinction of chairing sessions at divergent political platforms, like those of 'the Indian National Congress, the All-India Muslim League, the Jamiat Ulama-i-Hind and the Communist Party of India, which he helped found.'[11] He was a fascinating, multi-faceted person who was a Maulana, communist and poet, all rolled into one. He went on the Haj many times; and he also penned immensely romantic ghazals. His famous ghazal, '*Chupke choke raat din aansu bahana yaad hai/Humko ab tak aashiqui ka woh zamana yaad hai'* (I remember the days and night when I stealthily shed tears/I still remember those days of romance), has been a favourite of lovers across the subcontinent. But this verse, sung by the Pakistani ghazal singer Ghulam Ali, became immensely popular when B.R. Chopra used it in his 1982 film *Nikah*. The poems Hasrat composed while he was in prison shows how he took hardship on the chin. One couplet in a ghazal has become emblematic of what our freedom fighters went through in jail. Hasrat had to grind kilos of grain in jail, and he captured the essence of this tough task beautifully in a couplet: *'Hai mashq-e-sukhan jaari chakki ki mashaqqat bhi/ik turfa tamasha hai Hasrat ki tabiyat bhi'* (I am composing verse while moving the grinder/The mood of Hasrat is a wonderful spectacle). Hasrat was among the galaxy of prominent Urdu poets AMU produced.

With AMU turning a hundred, one is beholden to the MAO College Fund Committee's first meeting on 10 February 1873. The fund committee was formed a year earlier, in 1872. Addressing the meeting, Syed Ahmad Khan's son Syed Mahmood (1850–1903), had said: 'I think what we mean to found is not a College but a university, and I hope the members will consent to my proposal that instead of the word "College", the word "University" may be substituted.'[12]

Since the formal opening of MAO College was getting delayed, the fund committee began a school called Madrasatul Uloom Musalmanan-e-Hind on 24 May 1875 at Aligarh. The school was a precursor to MAO College, which metamorphosed into AMU in 1920, and during whose foundation-stone-laying ceremony on 8 January 1877, presided over by Viceroy of India Lord Lytton, Sir Syed had observed:

... this is the first time in the history of Muhammedans of India that a college owes its establishment not to the charity or love of learning of an individual nor to the splendid patronage of a monarch, but to the combined wishes and the united efforts of a whole community. It has its origin in causes which the history of this country has never witnessed before.[13]

So, what were the causes Sir Syed alluded to?

The large-scale killings and destruction in the wake of the failed 1857 Mutiny had unsettled Sir Syed, a judicial official in the East India Company. Muslims, who had borne the brunt of British repression heavily because the British held them responsible for the rebellion, had become fatalists. Irrationality, an obsession with obsolete and redundant social mores, rigidity in religious practices and a refusal to adapt to the new realities made them misfits in the era that the British Raj heralded. On close scrutiny, Sir Syed found that the reasons for the Muslims' unfathomable desolation lay mainly in their educational backwardness and resistance to modern, scientific thinking. Therefore, he saw a panacea for the community in modern, scientific learning. He began thinking about ways and means to bring his community out of the stupendous self-pity it wallowed in.

A visit to England in 1869 enabled Sir Syed to see first-hand the education system of the West, including that at Oxford and Cambridge. With the dream of an Indian college modelled on Oxbridge before his eyes, he returned to India and set out to realize that cherished dream. He quit his job in Benares and made Aligarh, then a small mofussil town 100 miles off Delhi on the Delhi–Calcutta route, his home. Since Sir Syed had saved several family members, including women and children, of some senior British officials during the 1857 Mutiny from Indian rebels and was among the defenders of British rule in India, no roadblocks in his path to founding his college remained permanent.

In Aligarh, he set up a residential college which would become the heartbeat of Muslims, as well as of a large swathe of undivided India. Alongside the college project, Sir Syed began the herculean task of social and religious reform. For this he established the *Tahzibul Akhlaq* or Mohammedan Social Reformer, a magazine in Urdu, which began hitting at the obscurantist, obsolete views that fettered the community. Other magazines were specially published to counter the views spread by the *Tahzibul Akhlaq*. Some of Sir Syed's religious views were unpalatable to the ulema and against accepted Islamic beliefs, and earned him the wrath of the orthodox elements in the community. He had to face the fury of fatwas. A maulvi even went all the way to Mecca to fetch a fatwa of kufr, declaring him an infidel. Sir Syed only chuckled at the serious drive to declare him a heretic, kafir or infidel, as it gave some of his tormentors an opportunity to visit Islam's holiest places. Sir Syed's debt to India in general and Muslims in particular lies not just in the college that he established but in the overall impact he left on the lives of Indians, especially Muslims.

Over 123 years after his death, Sir Syed is not considered a heretic, a naturi (one who propagated the belief that Islam is compatible with nature), a British stooge—epithets that some of his own community members hurled at him in his lifetime. Today, the orthodox ulema publicly say that Sir Syed, like any other person, is merely accountable to God for his lapses, and that his achievements and noble works outweigh his shortcomings and will pave his way to paradise.

Tomes have been penned on Sir Syed, MAO College, AMU and the movement Sir Syed and his associates like Mohsinul Mulk, Viqarul Mulk, Maulana Shibli Nomani, Maulana Zakaullah, Altaf Hussain Hali, Nazir Ahmad, and Chiragh Ali launched. This was called the Aligarh Movement, and it can only be described as the trigger for the Muslim renaissance in the subcontinent in late nineteenth and early twentieth centuries. It is easy to do a panegyric while evaluating the 100-year-long journey of a university which was born in the tumultuous times of India's freedom struggle of the 1920s.

The circumstances in which Jamia Millia Islamia came up deserve some detailing. In 1920, Mahatma Gandhi gave a call for the boycott of government and government-aided schools and colleges. Muhammad Ali opposed MAO College as it was pro-government, since it received government grants. Gandhi, Muhammad Ali and Shaukat Ali tried to persuade the pro-government elements at Aligarh to join the nationalist movement and turn the college into a nationalist institution. The pro-government group at Aligarh opposed the presence of Gandhiji and the Ali brothers at the campus as they were trying to persuade students to join their movement. On 12 October 1920, Mahatma Gandhi addressed the students and left. But the real drama happened on 13 October, when the Ali brothers suddenly appeared at a meeting being held at the students' union. Since they had been witness to Gandhiji being hooted and booed the previous day, the Ali brothers didn't speak but said they had only come only to say goodbye to the students of their alma mater. And they wept too because they had seen Gandhiji being booed. Present there was also Zakir Hussain, who had done his MA in economics from AMU and was a part-time teacher at the university. Zakir Hussain had arrived from Delhi the same day; he was running a fever and didn't want to speak. But he couldn't hold back his own tears when he saw the Ali brothers weeping. He stood up and declared that he had decided to resign from his teaching assignment at MAO College and forego the scholarship being given to him. This tilted the balance and changed the mood. Many students joined him in boycotting government institutions. In his biography *Dr Zakir Hussain*, M. Mujeeb, a colleague and friend of the professor, says that Hussain went to Delhi, where he met Dr M.A. Ansari, Hakim Ajmal Khan, Muhammad Ali and many others and 'assured them that a large number of teachers and students would leave the MAO College to join a national institution, if one was established. The leaders could ask for nothing better. On 29 October 1920, the Jamia Millia Islamia came into existence, and Maulana Mahmudul Hasan of Deoband delivered an address indicating its aims and ideals.'[14]

However, another version of the story is that Maulana Muhammad Ali had issued an ultimatum that he would establish another nationalist college if MAO College was not turned into a nationalist institution by 29 October 1920. On that date, Jamia Millia Islamia was founded at the Jama Masjid at Aligarh, at a meeting headed by Islamic scholar and freedom fighter Maulana Mahmoodul Hasan of the Darul Uloom Deoband.

Subsequently, on 22 November 1920, its board of trustees was created and the administrative set-up was given proper shape. Hakim Ajmal Khan became its first chancellor, Maulana Muhammad Ali became the vice chancellor and A.M. Khwaja, a contemporary of Jawaharlal Nehru's at Cambridge, its principal. Jamia, which emerged out of the enthusiasm of a handful of idealist students, initially ran out of temporary tents. The MAO college principal, Dr Ziauddin, initially closed the college, thinking that students would leave the campus and go home, but when he saw many had stayed back and were being poached by the nationalists, he reopened the college and tried to persuade the students who had joined Jamia to return to MAO College. He even wrote letters to the parents of his students to save their sons from being poached by the nationalist group. To clear the confusion about who belonged where, Dr Ziauddin gave an ultimatum to all the pro-Jamia Millia students to vacate the hostels. When they didn't, he called in the police and the college premises were cleared of the rebels. The Central Khilafat Committee financially helped the fledgling Jamia Millia. But after the abolition of the Caliphate in Turkey in March 1924, Jamia faced an existential crisis. In 1925, it was moved to a modest accommodation at Karol Bagh in Delhi. After a few years, three friends studying in Germany— Dr Zakir Hussain, M. Mujeeb and Dr Abid Hussain—returned to India to rescue Jamia Millia, which was on a ventilator by then. But that is a story for another book.

Sir Syed could have died in anonymity, as he had planned to after the holocaust of 1857, or enjoyed the fruits of his loyalty to the British, since he was offered a huge tract of land confiscated from a rebel nawab. He settled for neither and chose a third path, the path of a fighter who undertook the herculean task of spreading modern education and scientific thinking in his community. He preferred fight to flight. But 100 years after MAO College turned into AMU, that dream of Sir Syed is yet not realized. AMU has not achieved the goals that its founding fathers had dreamed of. This book is an attempt to point out the missed opportunities and the shortcomings that have fettered AMU from marching to the goalpost. If for millions it is the apple of their eye, it admittedly also gives heartburn to many. The book discusses why this is so.

This book is also my way of paying tribute to Sir Syed and the legacy he left behind, both in brick-and-mortar and thought and vision. I was a student of AMU for barely three years (1985–1988) and couldn't gather any certificate or degree. Barring the admission card issued to me—my prized possession—I have nothing else to prove that I ever studied there. I had joined the PCB (physics, chemistry, biology) section in the science stream in class eleven. I put my heart into my studies at first, but a few months later I realized I was not cut out for a career in medicine, which my father wanted me to pursue. I wanted to change my subject stream from science to liberal arts, as I wanted to study history, political science, English and other subjects in the humanities. I told my father about my desire to switch over from science to the arts as I aimed to crack the civil services exams and become an Indian Administrative Service (IAS) officer, but he would not listen. He reasoned that MBBS was a much easier target than the IAS, as AMU had a quota for the internal students (we will discuss the internal-external issue in the next few pages). He wept and sobbed back in his village even as I, at the leafy AMU campus, rebelled and began bunking science classes. I spent more time at the massive Maulana Azad Library with Khushwant Singh, M.J. Akbar, Kuldip Nayyar, Ghalib, Iqbal and Faiz Ahmed Faiz than in the physics laboratory. I religiously and voraciously read newspapers and magazines. They enhanced my English vocabulary—I had studied in Hindi medium till my matriculation—but didn't help me solve the question papers for physics and chemistry. My performance in the twelfth standard was so pathetic that my father pulled me out of AMU. I was barely fifteen or sixteen at the time, but I can't forget the day I reached Aligarh station to board the Magadh Express to Patna. Depressed, ashamed of my poor-performance, I cursed myself for not being courageous enough to change my stream from science to the arts on my own. Apart from 'wasting' three years, I had squandered my schoolteacher-father's hard-earned money too. I don't think I wept as much on the death of my parents as I did on the day I left Aligarh—defeated, desolate, depressed. This book is also to atone for those tears that rolled down that sixteen-year-old boy's cheeks.

Yet I owe my existence to AMU. Had it not been for the three years I spent there, I would not have been the person I am today. Aligarh taught me to defy the set norms, to think differently. I don't see it as a factory to produce degree holders. There are so many colleges and universities that award thousands of degrees and certificates annually. The AMU of my time was different; it inculcated a certain set of values that have stayed with me. It taught me to be respectful to my elders and kind to my youngers. It taught me to remain an optimist even when pessimism possessed me. I never sat for the civil services exam. However, AMU opened my eyes to the world and sowed the seeds of journalism in me. It introduced me to the wonderful world of literature.

A book on AMU has remained within me for decades. There may be a trigger that gets you to type out your thoughts on a computer, which then become part of a book, but the idea for the book itself germinates much ahead of its actual writing. It happened with me too. A book on AMU had to come out of me one day. I am glad it is coming out in the year I have turned fifty, as well as in a year when the AMU is celebrating its centenary, because the pandemic stopped the celebrations in 2020, keeping them low-key that year. The book is also the fulfilment of a promise I made to myself and to my three teenaged daughters.

This is a humble attempt to understand how Sir Syed's movement and his college, and then university, have impacted Indian Muslims. The shaping of the Indian Muslim mind has been a work in progress. AMU, by being the largest citadel of educated Muslims in the world, has contributed substantially to this making of the Muslim mind. I have tried to tell the story of the modern Muslim mind through the fascinating journey of AMU.

I must add, however, that no story of human progress and enterprise can claim to be final. And neither does this one.

1

The Making of AMU

ON 26 January 2021, after leading the Republic Day ceremony outside the red-brick Strachey Hall, AMU Vice Chancellor (VC) Dr Tariq Mansoor proceeded with the 'time capsule' committee members to the elegant Victoria Gate on the eastern side of the quadrangle that once formed the MAO College. Scaling down the majestic gate's stone steps, the contingent crossed the clean asphalt road and reached a spot in the park opposite the gate. In the next few minutes they created history. Here they buried a 30-foot-deep, 1.5-ton 'time capsule' containing the history of AMU, the names of its chancellors and vice chancellors from 1920 to 22 December 2020, Prime Minister Narendra Modi's speech at the online ceremony for the AMU centenary and many other memorabilia. 'This time capsule is for the benefit of future generations and it includes the salient features of the glorious history of AMU,' said Dr

Mansoor later, at an online function.'[1] Quoting the American philosopher George Santayana, the VC added: 'Those who cannot remember the past are condemned to repeat it.'

Mansoor was only following a precedent set more than 100 years ago, on 8 January 1877. Sir Syed's close friend and first biographer George Farquhar Irving Graham has described the foundation-stone-laying ceremony of the MAO college that he witnessed that year. After long speeches by Syed Mahmood (1850–1903), Sir Syed's son and the first Indian judge at Allahabad High Court, the Viceroy spoke and formally laid the foundation stone. 'A bottle containing scrolls and coins was deposited in a cavity of the foundation and a metal plate with a suitable inscription was placed over this.'[2] Graham returns to the foundation-stone-laying ceremony towards the end of the biography, *The Life and Work of Syed Ahmed Khan*. 'Under the stone are deposited a copy of the address given by Lord Lytton, enclosed in a bottle, some coins, and a short account of the ceremony engraved on a copper plate.'[3]

Dr Mansoor has formed a committee to excavate the capsule buried on that historic day in 1877. While it is yet to be found out if the capsule is in good condition after a century and a half, it is instructive to see if the college founded on that day has lived up to the expectations of its founders. Acknowledging the significance of the event, *The Pioneer* on 8 January 1877 had reported: 'The ceremony which takes place today at Allygurh marks the great progress already made by one of the most thoroughly sound and promising movements ever set on foot for the advancement of Indian education.'[4]

Before the foundation stone was laid, a sizeable number of guests, comprising nawabs, European officers and dignitaries from states like Punjab, the Deccan and Bengal, gathered at a delightfully decorated shamiana to witness history being made. There were elephants at the ceremony, as they were the mode of travel for many of the royals among the guests. Graham reports: 'On the outskirts (of the college grounds) were drawn up vehicles innumerable, and the presence of a few elephants with gaudy howdahs served to add to the general picturesque effect.'[5]

In his address, Lord Lytton called the ceremony 'an epoch in the social progress of India'.[6] He concluded his long speech with a prayer and wished the college 'Godspeed'.

But before we rediscover the giant Victoria Gate and the quadrangle that housed the college, comprising its boarding houses, Strachey Hall, Lytton Library, dining halls, museum and mosque, we must start from the beginning. How did the idea for the college come about?

In April 1869, Sir Syed took furlough from his sub-judge's job in Benares to travel to England. Accompanied by his two sons, Syed Mahmood and Syed Hamid, a close friend Khudadad Beg and his servant Chchajju, Sir Syed sailed for England from Bombay. His visit to England heralded a turning point in his life. In England he received the Star of India[7] honour, attended lectures, visited Oxford and Cambridge and private schools like Harrow and Eton. He was invited to private clubs and fabulous dinners. While reflecting on the progress Europe had made, he concluded that it was its modern education and scientific approach that had propelled the West onto the path of progress. And it was the lack of such an approach that had left India, especially its Muslims, backward. While in England, father and son (Sir Syed and Syed Mahmood) discussed the idea of founding a college in India. But before Sir Syed embarked on building a college, he wanted to prepare his *quam* (community) for the change.

Sir Syed had visited England for another purpose too. William Muir, governor of the North-West Provinces, had hurt the sentiments of Muslims with his work, *The Life of Mahomet*. Sitting at the India Office Library in London for endless hours, Sir Syed wrote a strong rebuttal to the work, exposing the many lies in Muir's assessment of the Prophet. To prepare his rebuttal, Sir Syed had to spend a lot on buying books. He wrote to his friends in India and asked his family to sell his personal library and send him money so that he could complete the rebuttal, which took the shape of a book named *Khutbat-e-Ahmadiya*.

In responding to Muir's book with another book, Sir Syed set a healthy example of civilized discourse. Instead of launching protests or calling for the author's head, he explained where Muir had gone wrong. He set an example for other Muslims too. But Muslims didn't learn much from Sir Syed. That was evident in their reaction to Salman Rushdie's *The Satanic Verses* in 1989, when Iran's spiritual leader, Ayatollah Khomeini, issued a fatwa of death on Rushdie. Though India was the first nation to ban the book, at least twelve people were killed and forty wounded after police fired on Muslim demonstrators who rioted en route to the British diplomatic mission in Bombay in February 1989. They were protesting against the British government which had sheltered Rushdie, then a British citizen. How would Sir Syed have responded? He would have written a rebuttal to Rushdie's book.

However, not all Muslims called for Rushdie's scalp. Scholar and former minister in Maharashtra, Dr Rafiq Zakaria rebutted Rushdie's book with his own book, *Muhammad and the Quran*.

Reviewing it in *India Today*, noted writer Khushwant Singh wrote:

> 'Zakaria's *Muhammad and the Quran* goes well beyond refuting Salman Rushdie's derogatory references to the Prophet and the Scripture. Its chief merit lies in a very lucid account of Muhammad's mission and, more than that, of his felicitous translation of selected passages of the revelations.'[8]

Dazzled by the new lights that he saw in England, Sir Syed deplored the darkness that engulfed Indians. There was not a day or night in England when India and the despondency in which the Indian Muslim lived didn't occupy his mind. His experience in England, writes Rajmohan Gandhi in *Understanding the Muslim Mind*, moved his focus 'from the present to the future.'[9]

Sir Syed returned to Benares in October 1870 after spending seventeen months in England. Within three months of his return, he launched the *Tahzib-ul-Akhlaq*, for which he had purchased stationery and got the blocks for its front page prepared. His letters from England had been published in the *Aligarh Institute Gazette*, the organ of the Scientific Society he had founded in 1864 in Ghazipur. Sir Syed subsequently moved to Aligarh after his transfer there. A section of Muslims didn't take very kindly to these essays—Sir Syed's unconventional, irreverent views did not go down well with them.

As soon as *Tahzib-ul-Akhlaq* hit the stands—its first edition appeared on 24 December 1870—it created a storm. Sir Syed not only wrote articles himself but also roped in like-minded writers to contribute to the periodical, which threw a rock into the still waters of Muslim intellectual life in the subcontinent. Altaf Husain Hali, a great admirer of Sir Syed's, a poet and Sir Syed's biographer too, has given a detailed account of Sir Syed's life and works, including the opposition to his views and the college project. In *Hayat-e-Javed*, the voluminous biography of Sir Syed, which was published soon after the subject's death, Hali says that Muslims opposed *Tahzib-ul-Akhlaq* vehemently. Fatwas were issued and Sir Syed was declared a kafir (infidel) and a Christian. Two magazines—*Noorul Afaaq* and *Noorul Anwar*—were issued from Kanpur to oppose *Tahzib-ul-Akhlaq*. Hali writes that people began opposing even those individuals who supported Sir Syed and contributed to his magazine. Maulvi Syed Mehdi Ali Khan, or Mohsinul Mulk, was among Sir Syed's ardent supporters. A story has it that someone went to Mohsinul Mulk's uncle, who was a Shia Muslim, and complained that Mohsinul Mulk had embraced Christianity and that his uncle should grieve. 'I wept the day he abandoned our sect [Shiaism] and joined your faith [Christianity],' said Mohsinul Mulk's uncle.[10]

Let us stay a little longer with *Tahzib-ul-Akhlaq*. This magazine heralded a new manner of writing prose in Urdu. Before Sir Syed, Urdu prose was hostage to fables and stories of kings and queens. It was complex and the emphasis was more on style than content. A lot of the writing in Urdu was of the religious variety. Sir Syed released Urdu prose from the trappings of ornamentation. The famous Urdu humourist and essayist Rasheed Ahmed Siddiqui aptly comments: 'Sir Syed's essays seem to have been written while seated not inside the abode of saints, but fighting life's battles.'[11]

Sir Syed had assembled a galaxy of literary stars around him. Mohsinul Mulk and Maulana Chiragh Ali were among those who contributed to *Tahzib-ul-Akhlaq*. Wordsmiths like Shibli Nomani, Altaf Hussain Hali, Maulvi Zakaullah and Deputy Nazeeer Ahmed joined what came to be called the Aligarh Movement.

Sir Syed's religious views didn't go down well with the orthodox ulema, of course.

Why were the orthodox ulema opposed to Sir Syed's religious views? To know the answer, I meet Abdur Raheem Kidwai, professor of English and director of both the UGC Human Resource Development Centre and K.A. Nizami Centre of Quranic Studies at AMU. He says that the ulema were opposed to Sir Syed because the latter rejected al-ghaib (paradise, miracles, shaitan, etc.), and didn't follow usul al-tafseer (principles of tafseer or interpretation of the Quran writing). He was not a trained theologian. His tafseer was not acceptable to the ulema then, is not acceptable to the ulema today.

He adds that Sir Syed's sincerity couldn't be doubted even if some of his religious views are 'unacceptable'. 'Why only traditional ulema? Even I feel Sir Syed should not have entered the territory he was not equipped to venture into. He was not a trained alim; neither had he undergone the rigour required to pontificate on such purely religious matters which concerned the faith,' he says.[12]

In a long essay, 'Quranic and Islamic Studies at the Aligarh Muslim University: An Assessment,' Kidwai maintains that Sir Syed's interpretations run contrary to the mainstream Muslim understanding.

His (Sir Syed's) later writings, especially *Tafsir* (interpretation of the Quran), however, have a specific agenda of pushing forward his social and educational reform programme. Prefaced to his *tafsir* is a set of

15 principles which he himself had formulated, and followed in his exposition of the Quran. It is worth clarifying that these principles have precious little in common with the centuries-old rich tradition of *usul al-tafsir* (principles of *tafsir* writing), professed and practised by Muslim scholars across the Muslim world.[13]

Sir Syed stirred the stagnant waters of the Muslim community and had both enemies and admirers. Even though they rejected his religious views, his admirers joined his mission. He and some of his adherents formed a 'Committee for the Better Diffusion and Advancement of Learning among the Mohammedans of India' on 26 December 1870. Sir Syed wanted to test the waters, and the committee announced an essay competition. The subject was 'Causes that prevent Muslims from availing of the benefits of government educational institutions and ways to reconcile Muslims to the western arts and science'. The Committee received thirty-two essays, and three prizes—first, second and third—were awarded.

According to chronicler S.K. Bhatnagar, who wrote one of the earliest histories of MAO College, three conclusions could be made from the essays the committee received: '1. Intelligent Muslims consider prejudice against Western education as ill-founded and harmful to Muslims, 2. The government will not be able to provide the right type of education for Muslims, 3. The Muslims should themselves provide for their modern education, which must preserve their cultural and religious beliefs.'[14]

The detailed conclusions of the Committee were sent to the Government of India and to the provincial governments of Uttar Pradesh (UP), Madras, Bengal and Bombay. The committee met at Benares and decided 'to look forward and to inaugurate an educational system for future generations'.[15]

The time had come for implementing the idea for the college Sir Syed had conceived in England. On 15 April 1872, the committee met at Benares and converted itself into the Muhammadan Anglo-Oriental College Fund Committee. It decided to publicize its decision to collect funds for the proposed college. Sir Syed became the committee's honorary life secretary.

Opinions were sought on the location of the college, and the fund committee, at its meeting on 10 February 1873, decided by forty-seven votes against five to locate the college at Aligarh. The committee, comprising lawyers, zamindars, judicial officials, Sir Syed, his two sons and one of his nephews, favoured Aligarh for several reasons. Sir Syed had taken retirement from judicial service at the Raj in 1876 and had settled in Aligarh. Aligarh was on the Delhi–Calcutta route of the railway that had opened in 1864, the year Sir Syed had founded the Scientific Society at Ghazipur before moving to Aligarh, and the Grand Trunk Road connected Aligarh with Delhi and Peshawar. 'Aligarh was away from any major river, so there were minimum chances of flooding during the monsoon. The water and air quality were good and convivial for health. It had a number of Muslim zamindars in the vicinity. Sir Syed, who had taken residence here after retirement, couldn't have got a better place to found his college,' says Rahat Abrar, former director of the Urdu Academy at AMU. 'Good, healthful climate was one of Aligarh's selling points,' writes author David Lelyveld.[16]

David Lelyveld sees another reason for Sir Syed's choice of Aligarh over other cities like Delhi, Allahabad and Agra for his college: 'Sayyid Ahmad, remembering the distractions of his youth, also wanted to avoid such major old cities as Delhi. He preferred a small town—accessible but also isolated. Students should not have contact with the outside world, especially the world of pigeon-keeping, kite-flying and courtesans.'[17]

Once Aligarh was chosen as the site for the college, the fund committee began to look for land. The parade ground of the Aligarh Cantonment was an ideal site for the college. The committee approached the government for a grant of 74 acres of land there. John Strachey, governor of the North-West Provinces, intervened and the government granted the land, with the condition that the Public Works Department would approve the buildings and the government could take back the land if it was misused. Sir Syed described the land in colourful prose as 'a piece of land in rich in brambles, ruled over by jackals and serpents.'[18]

The committee inaugurated the Madrasatul Uloom Musalmanan-e-Hind on 24 May 1875, with Maulvi Samiullah, a judicial official and Sir Syed's friend, presiding over the function. Samiullah was also the fund committee's secretary— Sir Syed was honorary secretary. Samiullah was a rich man, and according to Sir Syed, he could have enrolled his son Hamidullah in one of the best schools anywhere in India. Yet Hamidullah was among the first four students to enrol at the school. Seven teachers were appointed, and Oxford graduate H.G.I. Siddons was selected as the school's headmaster. Hali, who attended the inauguration, couldn't hide his happiness and described his high hopes for the fledgling institution in a poem. Those who accuse Sir Syed of being communal may note that among the seven teachers appointed for the school was Baijnath Prasad, on a monthly salary of Rs 120, even as

the salary of Headmaster Siddons was Rs 400 per month. The
school ran, but also faced difficulties as Sir Syed, the moving
spirit behind it, still held his job in Benares till July 1876.

Sir Syed took retirement in July 1876 at the age of sixty, after
thirty-seven years of service, which had enriched his life in
many ways.

Let us talk a little about Sir Syed's background. When Sir
Syed was born in 1817 in Delhi, Akbar Shah II (1760–1837)
was the Mughal emperor. Tracing his genealogy to Imam
Husain, grandson of Prophet Muhammad, Sir Syed's ancestors
belonged to Herat (Afghanistan) and had migrated to India
during Mughal Emperor Akbar's (1556–1695) reign. The
family maintained close links with the Mughal courts for nearly
two centuries, until almost the extinction of the once-mighty
Mughal rule in India. Sir Syed's grandfather Syed Hadi had
served both Alamgir II (1699–1759) and Shah Alam II (1728–
1806), becoming a Karori or revenue collector. Syed Hadi was
also a man of letters with a diwan (collection of poems) to his
credit.

Though Sir Syed's father Syed Muttaqi inherited all the titles
of the Mughal court, he was more inclined towards mysticism
and was a recluse.

More than his father, Sir Syed came under the influence of
his maternal grandfather Khwaja Fariduddin and mother Aziz-
al-Nisa. His mother taught him to be compassionate towards
the poor and respectful of elders. Once, his mother turned him
out of the house because he had slapped an aged servant.

It was in Fariduddin's house in Shahjahanabad (the area
known as Old Delhi today) that Sir Syed grew up. Fariduddin
served both the British and the tottering Mughal rule under
Akbar Shah, becoming his finance minister. Syed learnt Persian,

Urdu and mathematics at Fariduddin's post-dinner lessons. Subsequently, several teachers came home to teach him Persian and Arabic. Later he learned Arabic and some more mathematics from an uncle and aspects of Unani medicine from a family friend.

Sir Syed didn't learn English, nor did he join the Delhi College the Raj established in 1792 (today's Zakir Husain Delhi College) primarily because the Muslim elites, including the liberal Fariduddin, saw the British as terminators of the Mughal rule. By the time he turned eighteen, Sir Syed's education at home ended. He loved books and would often visit famous poets like Sahbai, Ghalib and Mufti Sadruddin Azurda.

Sir Syed read the writing on the wall early and, even if he had not joined the Delhi College or learned English, he bucked the trend and refused to join the decaying Mughal court. After the death of his father Syed Muttaqi in 1838, the Mughal Court's pension stopped. Despite strong opposition from family members, Sir Syed decided to work for the East India Company. He apprenticed under a relative at the Raj's court in Delhi, becoming first a reader and then a Munshi or junior judge. In the judicial service, he was transferred to many places in the United Provinces such as Mainpuri, Agra, Fatehpur Sikri, Ghazipur, Bijnor, Moradabad and finally Benares from where he took retirement in 1876.

Though he earned his bread from judicial service, Sir Syed burnt the proverbial midnight lamp to hone his writing skills. He helped his elder brother Syed Mohammed Khan in bringing out the Urdu journal *Syed-ul-Akhbar*. This early exposure to journalism helped Sir Syed become a pioneer in Urdu journalism (we will discuss it in the next chapters in detail). The sudden death of his elder brother in 1845 was a big blow to

Sir Syed. He shaved his hair, grew a beard and left the pleasure-loving company of young men in Delhi. He concentrated on his judicial job and writing, bringing out one remarkable book after another, including an unfinished commentary of the Quran.

In his youth, Sir Syed had enjoyed many games and hobbies, including swimming in the Yamuna. He used to visit the elite clubs of Delhi. Nothing appealed to him more than history, and he produced remarkable works like *Asarus-Sanadeed*, a history of some important buildings of Delhi, and his own edited versions of Abul Fazl's *Ain-e-Akbari* and Ziauddin Barani's *Tarikh-e-Firozshahi*. He approached the famous Urdu and Persian poet Mirza Ghalib (1797–1869) with a request to write the foreword (*taqriz*) to his edited version of *Ain-e-Akbari*. Ghalib reprimanded him in a Persian poem for squandering his time and energy on a dead past and suggested that he look up to the West, which was progressing with its inventions. Sir Syed didn't include Ghalib's poem in his foreword, though he had admiration for the poet.

Sir Syed was witness to the holocaust of 1857 and saw how it brought untold misery to Indians, especially Muslims, whom the British held responsible for the rebellion. He showed extraordinary courage when he wrote the *Risala Asbab-e-Baghawat-e-Hind* (Causes for the Indian Revolt). In the book he said that several wrong policies of the British had angered a section of Indians. Sir Syed suffered personally in the 1857 rebellion and its aftermath as his maternal uncle and a cousin were killed and his house in Delhi was looted. His old mother survived on the grains meant for horses for a week, as she had taken shelter at a stable near their house in Delhi.

So, the school and college of Sir Syed's dream were to create a sanctuary that would prepare generations of highly motivated youths who would be role models for the community. Sir Syed didn't want to compromise on quality, either in the teaching or in the materials used for building the college. When the British principal of the Roorkee College of Engineering refused to be the architect of the college in Aligarh, Sir Syed himself became its planner, designer and supervisor rolled into one. With the designs of Oxford and Cambridge in mind, he designed and planned the boarding houses, library, dining hall, a huge conference room named Strachey Hall, a museum and a mosque. In order to inculcate discipline among his students whom he saw as responsible and respectable future citizens, Sir Syed wanted to build a campus that was planned and majestic too. He wanted a space that would function as a community centre, and decided to build a self-contained quadrangle for it.

The construction work on the quadrangle proceeded in fits and starts. Work would halt when funds dried up and would resume when funds came from somewhere. If you look at the rooms at the residential halls—currently called Sir Syed South and Sir Syed North—they have the names of the donors inscribed above their doors.

Initially the plan was to construct two mosques, one for the Shias and one for the Sunnis. But ultimately, one mosque, called Jama Masjid, a prototype of the Jama Masjid in Delhi, was constructed. Abrar points to an old Arabic inscription in the mosque. It was taken from an abandoned tomb and had been done by a calligrapher who had worked on the Taj Mahal itself. This inscription decorates the outer wall of the mosque at AMU. 'On the northern side of the mosque's courtyard lies buried Sir Syed, who died on 27 March 1898.'

An MAO College principal who immensely influenced Sir Syed was Theodore Beck, a Cambridge graduate selected by

Syed Mahmood. Beck replaced Siddons, the first principal of MAO College, and took charge on 1 February 1884. Beck served the college for over fifteen years. Through amendments in the Trustees Regulation in 1889 and 1896, he became a formidable force as he not only controlled the college and the residential life of the students but also began interfering in Muslim politics. After all, he was a member of the All India Muhammadan Educational Conference that Sir Syed and his associates had started in 1886, a year after the birth of the Indian National Congress in 1885.

Sir Syed didn't oppose the Indian National Congress (INC) initially, though its demands—like admission of an increased number of Indians in the legislative councils and entry of more Indians in the Indian Civil Services (ICS)—riled him. He feared that Muslims would be outnumbered by Hindus in the councils and that the Bengali Hindus would bag the maximum number of seats in the ICS in an open competition. He asked Muslims to stay away from the INC and concentrate on education. Some blame Beck for misleading Sir Syed and dissuading him and his flock from joining the Congress. Sir Syed began actually opposing the Congress only after a prominent Muslim jurist of Bombay, Badruddin Tyabji (he founded the famous Anjuman-I-Islam in Bombay in 1874) was made the Congress president in 1887. About Beck's influence on Sir Syed, Bhatnagar says:

> Highly responsible persons hold the opinion that but for Mr Beck's personality the College would have remained a dwarf among the growing educational institutions. Other equally responsible people feel that the Muslims of India would have played a much more important role in the affairs of the country, and made a greater

contribution to freedom struggle had there been no Beck to influence Sir Syed in shaping the policies he later advocated.[19]

Many historians, including Rajmohan Gandhi, concede that in Sir Syed's last years it was Beck who ran the college, and this gave rise to the saying: '*Quam khuda ki, college Sir Syed ka, hukm Beck Bahadur ka*' (The quam is God's, the college Sir Syed's, the rule Beck's).[20]

Sir Syed's death in 1898 left Beck almost orphaned. He lost his zest for life, devoting himself to setting up the 'Sir Syed Memorial'. He toured extensively, giving lectures and raising funds. He wanted to set up a university in the memory of Sir Syed. He went to Shimla to recoup from an illness but died there on 2 September 1899. Beck loved MAO College so much that he had willed to have his grave carved in red brick, the kind of brick Sir Syed had chosen for his college. Fulfilling his wish, his tomb carries the English translation of an Urdu couplet: 'Man lays stone on stone to build a house and calls it my house. Neither mine, nor thine, but only a place of shelter for the birds to pass the night.'[21]

Later, the 'old boys' of the college are said to have collected a fund and built the hall of the Lytton Library, naming it 'Beck Manzil'. However, a biography of Sir Syed's by Iftikhar Alam Khan, a former head of the department of museology at AMU, carries a different account of Beck Manzil. The biography, *Sir Syed: Daroon-e-Khana* (Sir Syed: In His House) carries a presentation made by Sir Syed to the college trustees on 28 December 1891. Sir Syed says that a room near Strachey Hall was named Jubilee Room to commemorate the Jubilee celebrations of Queen Victoria. Khan says this room, after Beck's death in 1899, was named Beck Manzil.[22]

If Sir Syed ideated the MAO College, it was Beck who substantially helped create the 'Aligarh Boy' (the girls' school and college at Aligarh came much later). Though Beck was antagonistic towards both Hindus and the Indian National Congress, he never discriminated against Hindu staff or students at MAO College. Hali captured the communal harmony being practised on the campus during Beck's stewardship in the following verses:

Na dekhi hon jinhone Shafqat wa taat ki tasveerein
Woh Beck aur uske shagirdon ko baham hum sukhan dekhein
Na dekha ho jinhone par Hindu aur Musalman mein
Woh akar Muslim wa Hindu ko ek jaan wa tan dekhein

(If one has not seen the picture of affection and discipline/Let him come and see Beck and his students conversing with one another. If he has not seen love between Hindus and Muslims/Let him come here and see Hindus and Muslims as one soul in two bodies).[23]

Sir Syed's death on 27 March 1898 threw the college in the doldrums. In their essay 'The Campaign for a Muslim University, 1898–1920', scholars Gail Minault and David Lelyveld say that at the time of Sir Syed's death, the number of students at Aligarh College fell to 323 from 595 in 1895. 'This number further plummeted to 189 by July 1898.'[24]

Soon after the death of Sir Syed, the board of management of MAO College met on 31 March 1898 and decided to collect a fund of Rs 10 lakh to raise the college to a university. Aligarh old boys, along with Mohsinul Mulk as the main orator, toured the major cities of India, canvassing for subscriptions.

Mohsinul Mulk began to conduct sessions of the All India Muslim Educational Conference Sir Syed had founded in 1886, to promote modern, liberal education among Muslims, to shore up support for the university. At the educational conferences in Calcutta (1899), Madras (1901), Delhi (1902) and Bombay (1903), the demand for a Muslim university was discussed. Significantly, several influential Muslims were roped in to preside at the conferences in the major cities. So, the Calcutta conference was presided over by Justice Amir Ali, while Sir Aga Khan presided at the Delhi session and Justice Badruddin Tyabji at the conference in Bombay.

Meanwhile, the old boys, who had established their Old Boys' Association in 1889, introduced an innovation. Aftab Ahmad Khan, who as a student of MAO College had begun the 'Duty Society' to raise funds for the college by sending out students to 'beg', mainly during vacations, became a major figure in the Aligarh University movement. He had recently returned from Cambridge. 'At Cambridge, he decided that Aligarh would be centre of his life's work. Aftab was committed to the proposition that Aligarh was the vehicle to carry the Muslims into the world of modern ideas and liberal political institutions.'[25]

The association, led by Aftab, acquired the right to send three representatives to the board of trustees of the college. Aftab's group began holding annual dinners, where too funds were collected. The Sir Syed Memorial Fund Committee, the Old Boys' Association and the educational conferences began drumming up support for the university.

The entry of the Ali brothers—Shaukat Ali and Muhammad Ali—into the Old Boys' Association caused much friction in the association. It was now riven between Aftab & Co. and the Ali brothers.

The Ali brothers were interesting characters who went on to become great admirers of Mahatma Gandhi, with Muhammad Ali becoming the Mahatma's lieutenant in the Khilafat Movement of the 1920s. Raised singlehandedly by their mother Bi Amma, the widow of a courtier of the ruler of Rampur who had squandered his wealth in offering hospitality to friends and flatterers, the brothers first went to an English-medium school in Bareilly, moving later to the MAO College. The older brother Shaukat distinguished himself as a cricketer, becoming the college's cricket team captain, while Muhammad excelled in studies and oratory. Later, Shaukat joined the provincial civil services and funded Muhammad's education at Oxford. Muhammad appeared for the ICS exam but failed to clear it, returning to India with his BA in History (Oxford) degree. He wanted to teach at MAO College, but the British principal stonewalled his attempts as the British didn't want someone known for his fiery speeches and writings on the staff. He worked for the states of Rampur and Baroda. Muhammed later launched two papers—*Comrade* in English and *Hamdard* in Urdu—vehicles for his Islam-inspired nationalism.

In 1906, Aga Khan led a deputation of thirty-five leading Muslims to Viceroy Lord Minto in Shimla. Apart from asking for permission for Muslim representatives elected by Muslim votes in elected bodies, the delegation also submitted a memorandum demanding a Muslim university.

Hopes of a Muslim university were revived when Viceroy Lord Curzon (1859–1925) '... announced his approval of a Muslim University on condition that it was merely a continuation of the Aligarh College.'[26] But the Curzon-appointed Indian Universities Commission poured cold water on the proposals for the university, as it felt that the proposal 'did not have enough popular support or financial backing to make it viable'.[27]

Meanwhile, Muslim politics was moving at a fast space, even if the movement for the Muslim university had hit a roadblock. Within months of securing the Muslim vote, some Muslims formed the All-India Muslim League at Dhaka in 1906, with the Nawab of Dhaka chairing the opening session and Aga Khan becoming the League's permanent president. Muhammad Ali, though still working with the state of Baroda, was there too. Even if he was among the founders of the Muslim League, Muhammad Ali later claimed that he was a nationalist and would not compromise on Hindu–Muslim unity.

The factional dispute in the Old Boys' Association between Aftab's group and the Ali brothers widened. Muhammad Ali proved to be a constant thorn in the side of the European staff, especially of Principal William A.J. Archbold. Rajmohan Gandhi cites an interesting, testy face-off that took place between Muhammad Ali and Archbold in 1907, when the Ali brothers were students of MAO College. At Muhammad Ali's request, Congress leader Gopalkrishna Gokhale had been invited to address them.

Archbold declared the College out of bounds for Muhammad Ali, who refused to heed the order and was seen by Archbold near the College mosque.

Archbold: Don't you see the college is out of bounds for you?

Muhammad Ali: The College is my own. Who are you to impose any ban on my entry? Besides, I am standing at the door of the God's house.

Archbold: Remember, it will take me only ten days to return to England.

Muhammad Ali: It will take the same period for another Englishman to come out to India on the same salary.[28]

It was Aga Khan again who at the Muhammadan Educational Conference at Nagpur in December 1910 gave a 'Now or never' slogan for the Muslim university. Aga Khan headed the campaign and the Sir Syed Memorial Fund Committee was replaced by a Muslim University Foundation Committee. With Aligarh as its headquarters and Shaukat Ali accompanying him, Aga Khan toured India, collecting funds for the university.'[29]

Travelling in a special railway carriage, Aga Khan and Shaukat Ali collected substantial funds as they told people that colleges in different parts of the country would be affiliated to the Muslim university. And Muslims understood that their money would be used not just for one institution at Aligarh but to benefit the community members from other regions too. 'In five months, they received pledges for Rs 22,50,000 and actually collected nearly Rs 2,50,000. By August 1911, the amount pledged was Rs 25,00,000; the amount collected was nearly 4,00,000.'[30]

From here on the Muslim university became a fashionable cause. Following Aga Khan's campaign for funds, the Raja of Mahmudabad state in the United Provinces hired a train and toured Punjab and Sind. His party had, among others, Viqar ul-Mulk, Aftab Ahmad Khan and Maulana Shibli Nomani. Nomani had quit MAO College by then, but his intellectual reputation added weight to the university movement.

Subsequently, a constitution committee under the chairmanship of the Raja of Mahmudabad was formed to draft the constitution for the proposed university. The draft was submitted to Harcourt Butler, education member of the Viceroy's Council, at Shimla in May 1911. 'To the chagrin of the Ali brothers, Aftab Ahmad Khan was the spokesperson of the delegation that met Butler and the Ali brothers were left out.'[31]

According to the draft constitution, the main governing body of the university would be the court of trustees, composed entirely of Muslims, which would elect the twenty-five members of the executive council for three-year terms.

Butler wrote to J.P. Hewett, lieutenant governor of the United Provinces, that Muslims should be given their university.[32] Hewett agreed, seeing that since Muslims were so united in their demand it would be unwise not to acquiesce. But British control over the university would have to be much greater than what was provided for in the draft constitution.[33]

Though the Government of India submitted the draft constitution to London with recommendations that power of affiliation should be given to Aligarh, members of the India council opposed it. 'London also decided that the university should be called "The University of Aligarh", not "The Muslim University, Aligarh".'[34]

Since London was not ready to grant power of affiliation to AMU, it further fuelled disagreements between the Aftab Ahmad group and supporters of the Ali brothers. After the government passed the Benares Hindu University Bill on

1 October 1915, the pressure on Muslim leaders to accept the government's conditions for establishing the university mounted. In 1916, the Muslim leaders—at least one group—agreed to accept the government's terms for the university. The Raja of Mahmudabad persuaded leaders like Mohammad Ali Jinnah, Mazharul Haq and Dr M.A. Ansari to accept the university on the government's terms. But the Ali brothers further drifted away in regard to this matter. They would go on to play a major role in establishing another university—the Jamia Millia Islamia (JMI)—in 1920.

Hopes revived when Butler visited Aligarh on 19 November 1919. Luckily for the proponents of the Muslim university, Mian Mohammad Shafi, an old loyalist of Aligarh, became an education member in the Government of India. He helped expedite the Muslim University Bill. On 14 September 1920, the Aligarh Muslim University Act (1920) was passed, and it came into force on 1 December 1920. With the Raja of Mahmudabad as its first vice chancellor and the ruler of Bhopal, Sultan Jahan Begum, as its chancellor, the university was inaugurated on 17 December 1920 with a brief function at Strachey Hall. Muhammad Ali, never favouring the kind of university that the 1920 Act granted, lodged his dissent in his reply to the Raja of Mahmudabad's invitation to him for the inauguration. He wrote:

> I am painfully aware that it is not, as you state, 'The long-cherished dream of the Muslims', that 'has at last been realised' … Surely, Raja Sahab, this was not the university of your dreams any more than mine, nor can we call this the 'achievement of a grand and glorious undertaking' to which you and I had both set our hearts.

For had that been so, could we not have had our hearts' desire in 1912 instead of 1920.[35]

The promoters of Aligarh Muslim University failed in their attempt to get an autonomous network of Muslim educational institutions affiliated to AMU. Actually they wanted AMU to become a nucleus with an all-India status which would have many other institutions affiliated to it. But the British didn't agree to this plan. But the leaders of the movement went on to mobilize the community for their share in the political system. The movement trained the leaders to be persuasive, patient and focused on their goals. The fight for a Muslim university actually bore two universities: AMU and Jamia Millia Islamia, the latter being established in Aligarh on 29 October 1920. Five years later it moved to Delhi.

In the chapters ahead we will see how AMU influenced Muslim politics. We will discuss if it is truly what noted surgeon and AMU alumnus Dr Naseem Ansari had said: '*Aligarh (AMU) ko log Islam ka butkhana jante hain. Aur jahan ki mahfilon mein woh shamein roshan hain jinhein Taxila, Athens, Qartaba, Baghdad aur Oxford se laiye hain*' (People consider Aligarh as idol house of Islam. The light here that burns was brought from Taxila, Athens, Cordoba, Baghdad and Oxford).[36] Ansari wrote the *Jawab-e-Dost*, a book explaining in detail the nationalist and patriotic character of AMU. Ansari's book is a rebuttal of AMU alumnus and Pakistani civil servant (he migrated to Pakistan in 1948) Mukhtar Masood's book *Awaz-e-Dost*, a story of AMU from Pakistan's perspective in which it has been claimed that AMU created Pakistan.

2

Aligarh and Partition Pangs

MUKHTAR Masood studied from school (in one of AMU's sub-institutions) up to MA at AMU before his family migrated to Pakistan in 1948. He joined Pakistan's civil service and became a famous writer of Urdu prose. His books on Aligarh, though one-sided and written from a Pakistani perspective, are a tour de force and make for delightful reading.

Masood first met Mohammad Ali Jinnah at Aligarh in 1938. He describes the magnificent reception Jinnah received from students at the Students' Union Club that year. Never a great speaker, Jinnah, who spoke English fluently and was not comfortable with Urdu idioms and couplets—which most Muslim leaders then peppered their speeches with—had electrified the AMU students. Masood recalls:

He (Jinnah) seemingly lacked in the traits that were necessary for a Muslim politician. He had lived in London for years and was [a] stranger to many. He was not even a religious scholar and dressed like an English(man). He didn't know Arabic and Persian and not even Urdu ... His personal life was very lonely. His wife (Ruttie Petit) came into his life quite late (he was forty and she was just sixteen when they had married) and left early. He had a few friends and one daughter (Dina) whom he had disinherited (because she married Mumbai Parsi industrialist Nevile Wadia against his wishes). He had all the comforts of life.[1]

Not even once does Masood, an unabashed admirer of the Quaid-e-Azam (leader of the nation), mention his hero's well-known love of pork and whisky, both taboo in Islam. In fact, Jinnah's knowledge of Islam was not even rudimentary.

Scholar-politician and former minister of Maharashtra Rafiq Zakaria, in his book *The Man Who Divided India*, cites some interesting encounters that Jinnah had with some of his interlocutors, which show the scant regard the so-called Quaid-e Azam had for Islamic aesthetics. Once, after Independence, Jinnah readied to address an Eid congregation in Karachi. Zakaria writes:

Qazi Isa, a close associate of Jinnah, suggested to him that while addressing the Eid congregation he should recite a Quranic verse. Jinnah readily agreed and learnt one by heart. As soon as he finished his address he turned to Qazi and asked him whether he had recited the verse correctly. Excitedly the Qazi exclaimed, 'Alhamdollillah.' 'What does that mean?' Jinnah asked.

Isa said, 'It means Allah be praised.' 'Damn you,' Jinnah shouted. 'I did not ask you about Allah but about me.' The Qazi coolly assured him, 'You, my Qaid, are always right.'[2]

Another interesting incident occurred when freedom fighter-poet Maulana Hasrat Mohani (1875–1951), the man who coined the revolutionary slogan 'Inquilab Zindabad', went to see Jinnah without an appointment.

Jinnah was in his room and was as usual sipping whisky. He asked for the Maulana to be ushered in. Mohani, with his deep orthodox Islamic background, was taken aback to see Quaid-e-Azam drinking. Despite the anger seething within him, he composed himself. Jinnah saw the Maulana's face change colour. To humour him, he asked him whether he would like to taste the forbidden drink. 'No, thank you, Sir,' replied the Maulana, 'I have to answer my Allah.' Jinnah sensed his discomfiture. 'Maulana Saheb, I am a better Muslim than you. Unlike me, you have no faith in the mercy and benevolence of God.' Mohani spent a few minutes with his leader, acquainting him with the problems which troubled him and quietly went away, wondering whether all the sacrifices that pious Muslims like him had made in following Jinnah in the Pursuit of Pakistan had really been worth it. He felt betrayed with what he personally witnessed that evening.[3]

Jinnah came to Aligarh several times between 1938 and 1945. In 1938, when the AMU students gave Jinnah a rousing reception, the students' union had made him an honorary life member.

It was a tradition the union had followed since 1920, when Mahatma Gandhi was given this membership. In those days they would also put up a portrait of the guests they honoured on the Union Club's wall. It was such a portrait of Jinnah's at the AMU Students' Union Club that created a storm at the campus on 2 May 2018.

On that day, former diplomat, former Vice Chancellor of AMU and then Vice President of India M. Hamid Ansari was scheduled to visit the university on an invitation from the students' union for the same felicitation that many leaders had received at the Union Club since 1920. A day before Ansari's visit, the BJP member of Parliament (MP) from Aligarh, Satish Gautam, wrote a letter to AMU VC Professor Tarique Mansoor, demanding the removal of the Jinnah portrait from the campus. He also leaked the letter to the media.[4] A couple of Hindu right-wing organizations joined Gautam in demanding the taking down of the Jinnah portrait. Both the VC and the students' union said that the portrait had been hanging there since 1938, much before Partition. 'Who can deny that Jinnah came to Aligarh multiple times between 1938 and 1945. He gave a huge boost to the Muslim League's movement for Pakistan among the students of AMU. But we should also not forget that a large section of students at AMU then belonged to Punjab, Sind and Balochistan. Naturally, those students and teachers who belonged to these regions saw Jinnah as the deliverer of a new homeland, and they supported Jinnah and his two-nation theory,' says Shafey Kidwai, professor of mass communications at AMU and the university spokesperson during the time of the Jinnah portrait controversy that rocked the campus.

Around noon on 2 May, the car carrying Hamid Ansari and his wife Salma entered the Bab-e-Syed, the university's arched, red-stone main gate, and reached the portico of Guest House Number One (also called 'old guest house'). The students' union president, Mashkoor Usmani, a final-year student doing his bachelor's in dental surgery, and its secretary, Mohammad Fahad, along with a few others, were at the guest house to ensure that the day's chief guest was comfortably hosted. After tea and snacks, Usmani ushered the Ansaris to their room, promising to return after fifteen minutes when lunch was to be served at the guest house itself. The felicitation was to be a post-lunch event at the Union Club. A commotion began at the Bab-e-Syed, a mere 100 metres from the guest house where Ansari and his wife were put up. Usmani rushed to the gate, only to find that a dozen or so activists from Hindu right-wing outfits had barged in shouting provocative slogans and demanding removal of Jinnah's portrait. Usmani recalls: 'I was told that the first attempt to enter the campus by the activists was made at 11 a.m. They returned after Hamid sahab's arrival at the campus and forced their way through the gate despite the presence of police. Once they returned, we began demanding FIRs against the trespassers who had tried to disrupt the function where a former vice president was the chief guest.'

More students from the different hostels on the campus gathered outside the university gate and began demanding the lodging of FIRs against the trespassers. The students then moved towards Civil Lines Police station, located 500 metres from the main gate. The police lobbed teargas shells to disperse the crowd and began a lathi charge, injuring at least six, including Usmani. Usmani claims he was brutally beaten and fell unconscious. 'Instead of taking me to Jawaharlal Nehru Medical College and Hospital (JNMCH), an AMU entity on the campus, they took me to Malkhan Singh Zila Hospital, 5 kilometres away, for treatment. When I regained consciousness an hour or so later, I insisted on being taken to JNMCH. I told them I was a doctor and knew my proper treatment would not happen at the Zila Hospital,' says Usmani. For the next couple of weeks Usmani would come in a wheelchair, join the students' protest near the Bab-e-Syed on the campus and return to his hospital bed. Meanwhile, with the function cancelled, Ansari returned to Delhi that afternoon without getting drowned in rose and marigold petals from an opening in the roof of the Union Club's main hall. 'We had arranged for 100 kilograms of flowers for the ceremony,' says Usmani.[5]

When the chief guest stands to speak on the dais of the Union Club Hall, flower petals are thrown from an opening in the roof. It continues for several minutes, with the petals forming the pattern of flow of water. Ansari was denied this spectacular reception that afternoon. He was also scheduled to address the students at the Kennedy Auditorium, near the Maulana Azad Library, a few minutes' walk from the Union Hall. A few days later, Ansari wrote to the students' union president, praising the students for their protest. He added:

The disruption, its precise timing, and the excuse manufactured for justifying it, raise questions. The programme of the day, including an address by me in the Kennedy Auditorium, was publicly known. The authorities concerned had been intimated officially and were cognizant of the standard arrangements including security for such occasions. In view of it, the access of the intruders to close proximity of the university guest house where I was staying remains unexplained.[6]

The students kept up their protests for a couple of weeks, inviting national leaders and scholars to speak on communal amity and national integration.

The presence of Jinnah's portrait in the AMU campus gave some hardliners in the Hindutva camp a fresh handle with which to attack the university. It became a parameter by which to judge AMU's loyalty to India; which is why Prime Minister Narendra Modi's online address to the AMU community as part of the university's centenary celebrations on 21 December, where he called AMU a 'mini-India', silenced to an extent the habitual hatemongers who kept questioning AMU's patriotism by raising a trifling issue like the presence of a dusty portrait of Pakistan's founder on the campus.

But let us discuss how the Muslim League and its charismatic leader Jinnah received such huge support, from 1938 up to Partition in 1947, from the AMU community. A section of AMU had in 1920 backed Mahatma Gandhi's Non-Cooperation Movement, while another section certainly became passionate supporters of Jinnah and his Partition plan.

The 1937 results to the State Councils had been disastrous for the Muslim League, which won 108 of the 485 seats reserved for Muslims in the elections. The Muslim League garnered just 4.4 per cent of the total Muslim votes cast, obtaining 3,21,772 of the 73,19,445 Muslim votes cast. The performance of the Muslim League in the United Provinces was relatively better. It had won twenty-nine of the sixty-four Muslim seats in UP. In *Understanding the Muslim Mind*, Rajmohan Gandhi writes that after the elections, 'Jinnah had in mind a Congress–League settlement involving, among other things, power-sharing in the provinces.'[7]

While Mahatma Gandhi broadly agreed with Jinnah's proposal for a coalition government, at least in UP and Bombay where the League had done well, the Mahatma couldn't do much, saying 'I wish I could do something but I am utterly helpless.'[8]

In Bombay, Vallabhbhai Patel stonewalled the formation of a coalition as he wanted the League to merge with the Congress before its legislators became ministers, while in UP the talks broke down because of Jawaharlal Nehru, who called the shots in the Congress as its president in 1936 and 1937. Chaudhari Khaliquzzaman and Nawab Mohammad Ismail Khan were the leading lights of the Muslim League in UP. Before going to Patna to form the government there, Maulana Azad had spoken to both Khaliquzzaman and Ismail Khan and they had agreed to cooperate with the Congress and form the coalition government in UP, provided both were accommodated in the ministry. However, Jawaharlal Nehru wrote to both Khaliquzzaman and Ismail Khan, telling them that only one of them could be inducted in the ministry and the League should decide who that would be. But neither could come forward, as the popular sentiments in the League was that both deserved to be in the ministry. They rejected Nehru offer and this fuelled the allegations of the League that the Congress was not sincere in sharing power with the Muslims. This action of Nehru's was slammed by Maulana Azad. In seven states, including UP and Bombay, where the Congress won a majority of the seats, it formed governments without the League. This became a turning point in the history of India's freedom struggle, as League leaders began calling Congress-rule 'Hindu rule'. Maulana Abul Kalam Azad, in *India Wins Freedom*, observes:

If the UP-League's offer of co-operation had been accepted, the Muslim League Party would for all practical purposes have merged in the Congress. Jawaharlal's action gave the Muslim League in UP a new lease of life ... It was from UP that the League was reorganized. Mr. Jinnah took full advantage of the situation and started an offensive which ultimately led to partition.[9]

Rafiq Zakaria in *The Man Who Divided India* says that during this period Jinnah began aggressively advocating unity among Muslims. Zakaria writes:

During this period Jinnah had warned the Muslims that unless they were united, the Hindus, being the majority community, would subjugate them. He ridiculed Muslims who had thrown their lot with the Congress. They were traitors in Islam, he asserted, even if they were Muslims, the cause was greater than the individual. As for the rest of the Muslims, whether they were capitalists or paupers, zamindars or tillers of the soil, proprietors or workers and even exploiters, power-brokers [or] bloodsuckers, if they subscribed to his newly found anti-Congress stand, they were welcomed in his League. Jinnah's main aim was to bring all Muslims, irrespective of sect, class social position or economic status, under the League banner and mobilise the masses in order to present a united front against the Congress. He concentrated on making the League the only authoritative and sole organization of the Muslims. He wanted to parley with Gandhi on a basis of equality.

And his League to negotiate with the Congress on a one-to-one level.[10]

So, having been rebuffed by the Congress, Jinnah began advocating a 'separate nation' aggressively. Rejecting the celebrated poet Allama Iqbal's wish to have the 1937 session of the Muslim League in Punjab, Jinnah had it in Lucknow. Jinnah, whom the poet Sarojini Naidu had called 'ambassador of Hindu–Muslim unity', began seeking an 'exclusive' country for Muslims.

The October 1937 Lucknow session was so important to Jinnah that he discarded his well-cut suits and donned flowing trousers and a long coat. From Mr Jinnah, he transformed into Janab Jinnah and Quaid-e-Azam. While earlier he had kept himself aloof from ordinary Muslims, now he began mingling with them. His only regret was that he could not speak in Urdu.[11] Here we must look at how Jinnah raised the rhetorical slogan 'Islam in danger'. He travelled extensively, and Aligarh became a regular place to visit during these travels. Zakaria tells us that by now Jinnah had 'mesmerized' the Muslims. He writes:

> His (Jinnah's) charisma acquired irresistible force; regardless of his lack of knowledge of Urdu or the conventions, traditions or even rituals of Islam, he had so mesmerized the Muslims that they endearingly held on to every word he uttered without understanding it and listened to him spellbound and followed him faithfully. They revered him as a messiah who had come to their rescue. No saint could have asked for more.[12]

Jinnah and the League couldn't have found a better nursery than AMU, which Jinnah famously called the 'arsenal of Indian

Muslims'. In December 1938, Jinnah hurled perhaps his most lethal weapon at Gandhi when he described him as 'the one man responsible for turning the Congress into an instrument for the revival of Hinduism and for the establishment of Hindu Raj in India.'[13]

Leaders, AMU teachers and non-teaching staff sympathetic to the League played on the fear of 'Hindu rule' to the hilt. In Sir Ziauddin, the vice chancellor at AMU, the League found a great sympathizer who worked tirelessly to entice a huge number of students to the League. Journalist Tar Hasan writes:

> In February 1938, when Jinnah visited the campus, he was given a hero's welcome. The year 1938 at AMU campus was a turning point in the history of this institution. During the next seven years it was Jinnah and Jinnah alone who was calling the shots at Aligarh. Even as he was riding high at AMU campus, a determined group of Muslim nationalists at AMU and Jamia Millia were waging a battle to oppose the proposed partition of the country.[14]

Between 1938 and 1947 came the crucial year 1940, when at the annual session of the League in Lahore, Jinnah spoke in a language that had never been heard before. His presidential address showed that the League had reached a point of no return. He talked of fault lines between the Hindus and Muslims. Hindu organizations like the Hindu Mahasabha had only reaffirmed his belief that Hindus and Muslims were different and could not coexist and could not continue living in harmony. Disregarding their thousand years of coexistence and shared living, the polarizing patriarch declared:

It is extremely difficult to appreciate why our Hindu friends fail to understand the real nature of Islam and Hinduism. They are not religions in the strict sense of the word but are, in fact, quite different and distinct social orders, and it is a dream that the Hindus and the Muslims can ever evolve a common nationality, and this misconception of one Indian nation has gone far beyond the limits and is the cause of most of our troubles and will lead India to destruction if we fail to revive our notion in time. The Hindus and the Muslims belong to two different religious philosophies, social customs, literature. They neither intermarry nor inter-dine, and, indeed, they belong to two different civilisations which are based mainly on conflicting ideas and conceptions ... To yoke together two such nations under a single state, one as a numerical minority and the other as a majority, must lead to growing discontent and final destruction of any fabric that may be so built up for the government of such a state.[15]

The Congress tried to explain the untruths that Jinnah had spoken. It had no better weapon in its arsenal to respond to Jinnah's espousal of the two-nation theory through propaganda and a dangerous reading of India's civilizational history than Maulana Abul Kalam Azad. Gandhi and Nehru depended a lot on Azad and hoped that this man, who had mesmerized his quam with his powerful pen and eloquent oratory, would dissuade Muslims from biting the bait that Jinnah had laid. Azad was at his eloquent best at the Ramgarh session of the Congress in 1940. This was a clarion call to his co-religionists not to abandon the Hindu–Muslim unity that had characterized India for centuries. Azad argued:

> It was India's historic destiny that many human races and cultures and religions should flow to her, finding a home in her hospitable soil, and many a caravan should rest here ... One of the last of these caravans, following the footsteps of its predecessors, was that of the followers of Islam. This came here and settled here for good. This led to a meeting of culture-currents of two different races. Like the Ganga and Jamuna, they flowed for a while through separate courses, but nature's immutable law brought them together and joined them in a sangam. This fusion was a notable event in history ... Eleven hundred years of common history have enriched India with our common achievements. Our languages, our poetry, our literature, our culture, our art, our dress, our manners and customs, the innumerable happenings of our daily life, everything bears the stamp of our joint endeavour. His [India's] joint wealth is the heritage of our common nationality and we do not want to leave it and go back to a time when this joint life had not begun ... The cast has now been moulded and destiny has set its seal upon it. Whether we like it or not, we have now become an Indian nation, united and indivisible. No fantasy or artificial scheming to separate and divide can break this unity. We must accept the logic of fact and history and engage ourselves in the fashioning of our future destiny.[16]

However, the Congress must share the blame for failing to take strong measures to convince the Muslims that Partition would not be in their favour. Neither the pro-League section in the AMU community nor Muslims elsewhere in the country were made to understand that the split in the community would leave the majority of Muslims in the lurch. Zakaria directs his barbs against the Congress in no-holds-barred manner:

> The Congress, like the ostrich, buried its head in the ground to the growing separation trends which Jinnah fostered. After his eloquent peroration, Azad withdrew into a shell instead of boldly confronting Jinnah by going to the Muslim masses and awakening them to the dire consequences of such a dangerous demand. He swallowed even Jinnah's characterisation of a 'showboy of the Congress'. His colleagues did not bother to snub Jinnah for insulting their president. He (Jinnah) was pilloried only by Hindu-owned press which Jinnah exploited to portray himself as a martyr before the Muslim public. There was no concerted rational approach on the part of the Congress to expose Jinnah's game which threatened to put Hindus and Muslims at loggerheads and thus to undermine the composite character of a nation.[17]

Sir Ziauddin was an alumnus of MAO College, a noted mathematician who had even qualified for the deputy collector's job in the provincial services. But at the behest of Sir Syed, he decided to go for academics and became a teacher at Aligarh, the university's first pro-vice chancellor and later its vice chancellor. Dr Rahat Abrar, who has written about

Aligarh extensively, says that Sir Syed was at his residence when Ziauddin went to him to break the 'good news' that he had qualified for the provincial services, hoping Sir Syed would congratulate him. Instead of showing happiness, Sir Syed asked Ziauddin to bring him the lock and key that he had placed in the room some distance away. 'Giving the lock and key to Ziauddin, Sir Syed asked him to go and lock the college's gate because there was no reason to run it [the college] if brilliant students like him left him. Ziauddin gave up the idea of taking up the government job and instead continued in the college, becoming its VC after it became a university,' says Abrar.

Aligarh became a big laboratory that supplied a young, emotionally charged youth brigade to back the two-nation theory. Ziauddin, who became Sir Ziauddin after he was knighted, became Jinnah's biggest supporter at Aligarh. He began influencing students to support the Muslim League's demand for Pakistan after the League passed a resolution for a separate nation at Lahore in 1940. Though the 'nationalist group' at Aligarh was ridiculed, humiliated and pooh-poohed by the 'pro-Pakistan' section at Aligarh as they were outnumbered by the aggressively dominant League sympathizers, the 'nationalists' refused to be cowed down. Prominent among the 'nationalists' were the noted historian Mohammad Habib (father of Irfan Habib, a leading historian of India today), history teacher A. Halim, Urdu humorist and author Rasheed Ahmed Siddiqui, Abdul Majeed Khwaja, Ziaul Hasan Farooqi, Habibullah Azmi and Ashfaq Azmi. But nothing could surpass the humiliation freedom fighter, scholar of Islam, orator, writer and Quran commentator Maulana Abul Kalam Azad suffered at the hands of the Aligarh boys.

In the summer of 1945, Maulana Azad was travelling to Calcutta from Delhi by the Kalka Mail. The pro-League students of AMU, having heard that Maulana Azad was on the train, mobbed it at Aligarh station. Fortunately, Azad's fellow passengers closed the door of the compartment in which they were travelling. For an hour or so, the train remained held up at Aligarh station. The students might have lynched Azad had his co-passengers not stopped him from going out of the compartment and facing the 'mob'. The train moved only after some senior teachers intervened.

Hasan describes how the 'loyalist group', led by Sir Ziauddin, was disillusioned after it became clear that in the new country of Muslims Aligarh would have no role. Some Muslim League leaders had misled the boys at AMU into believing that after Pakistan was created, a corridor would link East Pakistan and West Pakistan and that Aligarh would fall along this corridor. By the middle of 1945 it became clear that the promise of such a corridor was false. Sir Ziauddin began distancing himself from Jinnah, and Jinnah stopped visiting Aligarh.

The students who had earlier adored Sir Ziauddin now began to be critical of him. Sir Ziauddin, who, at the beginning of the academic session of the university in 1937 had said that every individual in the university had the full right to join any political party, now held a closed-door meeting at Strachey Hall with the teachers in April 1945. He told the teachers that the corridor was a pipe dream. '... Aligarh would now have to totally review its political line because he was convinced that in the proposed Pakistan, Aligarh would have no role,' writes Hasan.[18]

When the students heard of the meeting they began gathering outside the hall. When Sir Ziauddin came out of the hall he was manhandled. The mob charged at him, but somehow the VC locked himself inside a toilet. Some senior teachers intervened and he was persuaded to come out of the toilet. The mob was pacified only after Sir Ziauddin resigned. It was Ziauddin as principal of MAO College who had called in the police to get some nationalist students vacated from the AMU hostels. He did not want them to stay on the campus as their loyalty had changed to the new, nationalist institution (Jamia Millia) they were about to create.

The man who was once the darling of AMU students now quit the institution and went to England, feeling deeply sad and humiliated. He died on 4 January 1948. According to his wish, his body was brought to India. Despite resistance from the staff, the students buried him beside Sir Syed's grave in the Jama Masjid premises. Partition had happened and the pro-Pakistan students had either left the campus or changed their stand and acknowledged the services Sir Ziauddin had done for the institution, as teacher, principal of MAO College and VC of AMU. And he had not gone to Pakistan. Many years later another vice chancellor, Ali Yavar Jung, would face another mob of students in 1965 and escape from the jaws of death. Having sustained thirty wounds on his head after a student flung an iron rod at him, Jung resigned under threat to his life. This will be discussed in detail in the coming chapters.

Hasan writes:

> ... (Sir Ziauddin's) 'final moments of anguish and despair' ... '(are a) reflection of the despair and frustration suffered by Muslims of UP and those belonging to other Muslim minority states. It was the culmination of a series of political blunders made both

by the Congress and Muslim League leaders—men like Chaudhary Khaliquzzaman and Liaqat Ali Khan. In the eyes of many the dream of Pakistan had turned into a nightmare even before it came into existence.[19]

After Sir Ziauddin's resignation on 24 April 1947, Mirza Mohammed Ismail Khan, a League leader, became the acting VC. He continued in his post till a former Aligarh student and one of the founders of Jamia Millia Islamia, noted educationist Dr Zakir Hussain, was plucked out from Jamia to 'save' Aligarh and was appointed its VC. Dr Hussain agreed to take up the assignment on the condition that the university court elected him, as he would not go there as the government's nominee. The court held a meeting on 28 November 1948; acting vice chancellor Nawab Muhammad Ismail Khan resigned and Dr Zakir Hussain's name was proposed. Accepting Nawab Muhammad Ismail Khan's resignation, the court elected Dr Zakir Hussain as the new VC. On 29 November 1948, AMU opened a new chapter for itself in newly independent India.

3

The Inheritor of Sir Syed's Legacy

BEFORE we move to the post-Partition era of AMU, we must look at the life and times of Sir Ross Masood, Sir Syed's only grandson, an AMU vice chancellor who had infused the campus with scientific temperament. He is the one about whom the poet Hali said 'Sir Syed had donated [him] to the community'.

The night was dark and cold. A man took his teenaged son to an orchard near his house in Aligarh and began teaching him how to plough. The boy's mother panicked and sent for a family friend to bring the boy home. The friend covered the shivering boy under his warm overcoat and had him sent home. The friend then spent rest of night listening to the boy's father's lecture on the need to promote agriculture in India.

The boy was Ross Masood, son of Syed Mahmood and the only grandson of Sir Syed. The family friend who rescued the boy from his torturous 'education in agriculture' was the MAO College British principal, Theodore Morison. On Ross Masood's mother Musharraf Jahan Begum's request, Morison took custody of the boy. Masood would grow up into a tall, handsome man who epitomized class, dignity, decorum and intellectual integrity. A true product of the Aligarh Movement, he carried the best values of the East and the West. Knowing Ross Masood is akin to understanding the Muslims of India in the crucial period of the second and third decades of the twentieth century. As vice chancellor of AMU (1929–1934), Ross Masood embarked on fulfilling the vision of his grandfather, Sir Syed, who had said with great hope, 'Science shall be in our right hand and philosophy in our left; and on our head shall be the crown of "There is no God but Allah and Mohammad is His Messenger".[1] As the only grandson of Sir Syed who had imbibed the values the grand old man of Aligarh epitomized, Masood represented the modern, forward-looking community Sir Syed had striven to create. It therefore makes sense to know the man and his work in some detail.

Born on 15 February 1889 at Sir Syed House, the beautiful bungalow in Aligarh Syed Mahmood had bought from the British army officer H.D. Ferguson for his father in 1876, Ross Masood was the apple of Sir Syed's eye. Sir Syed would play with the child, sing lullabies to him, put him on his chest, carry him on his back and laugh at the boy's tantrums. Syed Mahmood was sixteen years older than Musharraf Jahan Begum, who was also known as Begum Mahmood. She was the daughter of Nawab Khwaja Ashrafuddin, a descendant of Sir Syed's maternal grandfather Khwaja Fariduddin Ahmed Khan. The wedding of Syed Mahmood and Musharraf Jahan Begum on 28 February 1888 was a grand affair at MAO College. The walima (a feast hosted by the groom's family) on 5 March 1888 was held at the massive dining hall in Salar Manzil at the college quadrangle. While the bridegroom donated Rs 500 to the college, its Persian teacher and noted poet Shibli Nomani sang a qaseeda or eulogy on the occasion.

Firstly, the name 'Ross' for a Muslim child was unusual and almost scandalous for the times. George E.A. Ross and Syed Mahmood were close friends, both in England and at Allahabad where they practised law. It was the Ross couple who gave their name to the child. Sir Syed acknowledged the couple's love and favour at the child's 'Bismillah' (ceremony where a Muslim child begins learning the first letters) which was celebrated with much fanfare at Strachey Hall. The ninth session of the All-India Muslim Educational Conference was held on 27, 28 and 29 December 1893 at the under-construction Strachey Hall, and Masood's Bismillah took place on 30 December at the conference's conclusion. Usually, on such occasions the child is placed on the lap of a close senior relative, but Sir Syed wanted to send a message and ensured that Ross Masood sat on the lap of Raja Jaikishan Das (1832–1905), a close friend of Sir Syed. Sir Syed had gifted Rs 500 on behalf of Ross Masood to the college's fund. Addressing the crowd, which had Muslim, Hindu and Christian invitees, Sir Syed said:

> Friends, I have always spoken about my quam or community but that doesn't mean that I don't like other communities. My community is in dire straits and so I mostly speak about it but I love other community members just as I love my own people. Right now, there are two examples of this. One is that Syed Mahmood and Mr Ross (George F.A. Ross) are great friends. When

Ross Masood was born, Mr. and Mrs. Ross gave their name to the newborn boy. We accepted their offer with happiness and added it to his name and his name became Ross Masood. The second example is my friend Raja Jaikishan Das. He is like my brother. Syed Mahmood calls him chacha or uncle and Ross Masood calls him Dada Raja. I love my friends and don't discriminate against them.[2]

Raja Jaikishan Das gifted Rs 500 to Masood, which was donated for the construction of Strachey Hall. Sir Syed's 'donation' of his only grandson to the community, as mentioned by poet Hali, the patriarch's biographer, happened at this ceremony.[3]

Years later, on 20 October 1929 to be precise, Ross Masood reached Strachey Hall again. This time he was not on anyone's lap, but destiny had given him a chance to steer the seat of learning his grandfather had founded.

Years ago, Masood was at Strachey Hall before his departure in 1906 for England for higher studies. He graduated from Oxford and did his bar at law from Lincoln's Inn. In 1906, Ross Masood and two others (Haroon Khan Sherwani and Abdur Rashid Khan) were given a send-off at Strachey Hall. College secretary Mohsinul Mulk congratulated the three boys readying to embark on a new journey. A big feast was held in honour of the three 'star students' from MAO. It was Masood who spoke on behalf of the three and thanked the college committee for the fabulous farewell. Neither Masood nor his classmate at MAO College and Oxford, Abdur Rashid Khan, would have imagined that one day Masood would marry Rashid Khan's daughter Umtul Rashid Begum. But we will return to that marriage a little later.

Much water had flown down Aligarh's old kathpula (wooden bridge which connected the university to the old city) since Masood's Bismillah ceremony in 1894 and farewell in 1906. It was 1929, and by then Strachey Hall had hosted innumerable guests, including viceroys, lieutenant governors, heads of states, celebrated scientists, noted poets and writers. MAO College, which metamorphosed into Aligarh Muslim University in 1920, had fallen on bad times. Groupism among teachers and other staff sapped it of energy even as paucity of funds threatened to throttle its growth. AMU needed dynamic leadership that could help it paper over these crises. Ross Masood had by now distinguished himself as a leading educationist after quitting the law practice. He had years of experience and a burning desire to serve his alma mater. As the headmaster of a government school in Patna, as a history teacher at Renshaw College at Cuttack in Orissa (Dr Rajendra Prasad, who became India's first President, was a fellow teacher here), and as director of education in Hyderabad state, Ross Masood had distinguished himself as an educationist and administrator.

In the twelve years (1916–1928) that he was director of education at Hyderabad, Ross Masood brought many reforms in the state's education system. Among other things that he will be known for in Hyderabad's history, the creation of Osmania University stands out. Along with the secretary of education at Hyderabad, Syed Akbar Haideri, and Baba-e-Urdu (Father of Urdu) Maulvi Abdul Haq, Ross Masood piloted the university project. It was India's first university with Urdu as the medium of instruction. Even the science subjects were taught in Urdu, and Hyderabad's Darul Tarjuma (House of Translation) was tasked to translate well-known books from English to Urdu. However, the scientific terms accepted globally were retained in the Urdu textbooks, so as not to inconvenience the students once they went for higher studies or into jobs.

Hakim Syed Zillur Rahman, in his book *Ross Masood*, cites an interesting incident before permission to found Osmania University was granted in 1918. One day Maulvi Abdul Haq, who had been trying to get the necessary papers to start the university signed by the state's British resident, approached Ross Masood. The resident was not very keen on greenlighting an Urdu-medium university. Knowing that Sir Syed was Ross Masood's hero, Haq told Masood that he had to prove that he was Sir Syed's grandson. 'How?' asked Masood. 'Get me the necessary papers for the university signed by the state's resident,' replied Haq.[4]

Ross Masood went to meet the British resident at Koti Residency, the opulent mansion in Hyderabad that James Achilles Kirkpatrick, the British resident of Hyderabad between 1798 and 1805, had built.[5] Since Masood could speak French as well as English, he began conversing with the resident's children in French. The resident told Masood he could speak in French to him but not to the children as they were more comfortable in their mother tongue (English). 'Just as your children are getting education in their mother tongue, we too want our Muslim children to get education in their mother tongue ... When they grow up, they will learn English, French, German or whichever language they want to learn ... ' Masood told the resident, finally convincing him to sign the necessary papers.[6] And Osmania University came into existence. Sir Syed had once dreamed of creating a vernacular university in India. With Osmania University seeing the light of day, his grandson Ross Masood had realized the grand old man's dream of establishing a vernacular university.

While still with the princely state of Hyderabad, Ross Masood took six months' leave to travel to Japan to study the education system there. He spent over three months in Japan, visiting schools, colleges and universities, and meeting people to understand the reasons for Japan's progress. On his return Masood prepared a detailed report on the education system in Japan. He returned to Japan in 1925, and this time he also travelled to Korea and China. His faith in education through the mother tongue only strengthened after his two visits to Japan. He also began to believe in free primary education.

You can take an Alig (alumnus of AMU) out of Aligarh but cannot take Aligarh out of an Alig, goes a saying. Aligarh beckons its alumni time and again. There are stories of old boys and girls returning to the campus and weeping on visiting their hostel rooms decades after they had left. Perhaps no founder of a university gets remembered with so much euphoria and enthusiasm on his or her birthday as Sir Syed. His birthday (17 October) is celebrated as 'Sir Syed Day' by Aligs across the globe. The Sir Syed Day dinner is the celebration's main attraction, where Aligs eat together as they remember the university's founder and the traditions they imbibed on the campus. One of the delightfully memorable occasions at AMU is when the students' union invites a distinguished guest and felicitates him or her with the conferment of honorary life membership of the union. The students of AMU invited Ross Masood for this membership and felicitation on 21 December 1924. Flowers rained on him as he stood up to speak. He was toasted with speeches and panegyrics in verse. But this visit of his to AMU was as a guest.

Ross Masood's first visit to AMU after his appointment as its vice chancellor was also memorable. After quitting his service with Hyderabad state in 1928 on health grounds, Masood went to Europe to recuperate. He had planned to settle there and had even acquired a house in Paris. But Aligarh beckoned him again. Before we move ahead, it seems relevant to discuss the financial condition of Sir Syed's family. Sir Syed neither inherited huge ancestral properties nor owned tracts of land or businesses. His maternal grandfather's haveli where his mother lived was looted in the 1857 mutiny. He survived on the salary (beginning from Rs 100 and going up to Rs 800 per month when he retired after thirty-seven years of service) he received from his judicial service (pension Rs 600 per month after retirement in 1876). When his son Syed Mahmood passed matriculation in 1867, he was granted a scholarship—the first of its kind in the North-Western Provinces—to study in England. The Provinces' lieutenant governor, William Muir, had recommended his name for this scholarship. The government of India had granted nine scholarships for Indian students to study in England and Syed Mahmood was the only student from the North-Western Provinces. He was granted Rs 3,000 for the travel and Rs 6,000 annually for his stay in England.

Sir Syed saw this as a great opportunity to visit England. In his leave application, Sir Syed said that he would benefit immensely from this visit and also informed the fellow countrymen about the progress England had made. He wanted to see the education pattern in England, especially at Cambridge and Oxford, and wanted to write a rebuttal to William Muir's book on the Prophet. He had to face immense difficulties in collecting funds for his journey to England. He sold his library, mortgaged his old house and property and borrowed money from friends and even moneylenders at a very high rate of interest to fund his journey to and stay in England.

Syed Mahmud became a famous lawyer and later judge of the Allahabad High Court. He was so prosperous that he bought a military officer H.D. Ferguson's house for Rs 6,000 for his father in Aligarh. He redesigned it in European style. Sir Syed hosted many viceroys, lieutenant governors, princes, nawabs and maharajas at this house where he lived for twenty-two years till a few days before his death. This is called Sir Syed House and today Sir Syed Academy is housed here. He later had to move to a friend's house because of the erratic behaviour of Syed Mahmood who had lost mental balance.

Syed Mahmood's son and Sir Syed's grandson Ross Masood's initial education happened under the guidance of his mother Musharraf Jahan. MAO College's third principal Theodore Morison took Ross Masood in his custody as Syed Mahmood's erratic behaviour was not conducive for the growth of Ross Masood. Like his father, Ross Masood too got a scholarship for higher studies in England. Begum Mahmood didn't want to send her son to England but the lieutenant governor of the North-Western Provinces, Sir James Latouche convinced her that the Government of India would bear the cost of his education in England. Ross Masood left Aligarh in 1906 for England for higher studies. We have earlier seen how Theodore Morison, who by now had retired from MAO College and returned to England, became Ross Masood's local guardian in England.

Ross Masood returned to India in 1912, practised law at Patna High Court but quit it and joined education service. He later became director of education at Hyderabad before joining AMU as VC and later minister of education at Bhopal state (we have discussed it in this chapter). By now he was a rich man and could afford to live anywhere in the world.

As mentioned earlier, before Masood took charge as VC, the university had gone through a tough time. Groupism and corruption had tarred its reputation, so much so that the chancellor—the ruler of Bhopal, Sultan Jahan Begum— appointed the Rahmatullah Committee to inquire into the ills that bedevilled the university. The chancellor also wrote a long note in Urdu about the need for the inquiry committee. In the note she observed:

I don't need to keep emphasizing how much I love AMU. We have not been able to realize the dream of Sir Syed. Regrettably, we have not turned Aligarh into the Qurtaba (Cordoba) of the east. We are wasting our energies in internal fights and differences, which are taking us away from our goal.[7]

Sultan Jahan Begum's reference to Cordoba, that historic city of Muslim Spain, has a significance. And for valid reasons. Let us see how. After the overthrow of the Ummayad dynasty by the Abbasids in 750 AD, Abdur Rahman, a dashing young Arabian prince, came to al-Andalus (Arabic for Iberia). Abdur Rahman's dynasty, which culminated with Abdur Rahman III, created a glorious period in European history. Akbar S. Ahmed, former Pakistani ambassador to the UK and Ireland and currently the Ibn Khaldun Chair of Islamic Studies at American University in Washington, DC, has visited Cordoba many times. In his critically acclaimed book *Journey into Europe: Islam, Immigration and Identity*, Akbar Ahmed captures the scintillating beauty of the ruins of the town Madinat al-Zahra on the outskirts of Cordoba. 'Built by Abdur Rahman III, it was a glittering town that dazzled visitors. The architecture and town planning were breathtaking, and evidence of it can still be seen.'[8] But what is more impressive than their beautiful buildings, observes Akbar Ahmed, is the Andalusian model of La Convivencia or a pluralist society that Abdur Rahman and his successors created, ' ... encouraging acceptance of others and the pursuit of knowledge, art, literature.'[9] No talk of Cordoba can be complete without the mention of the Masjid-e-Qurtuba or the Grand Mosque of Cordoba, now the Catholic cathedral of the Diocese of Cordoba. In 1933, Allama Iqbal, the poet-philosopher and great friend of Ross Masood visited Spain and also went to see the Grand Mosque of Cordoba. The most important spot in a mosque is the arch of the mehrab, the designated place which points to Mecca. Akbar Ahmed writes: 'I recalled that Allama Mohammad Iqbal, the celebrated Muslim poet-philosopher, had bowed in prayer at precisely this spot and in one of his most popular poems, *The Mosque of Cordoba*, declared, "You have elevated Andalusia to the eminence of the Haram (in Mecca)".'[10]

It was that kind of eminence that Sultan Jahan Begum wanted Aligarh to reach. She also mentioned the ideals that AMU stood for—large-heartedness, pure morality and free thinking—which the AMU community had forgotten. The inquiry commission recommended, among other steps, the removal of Dr Ziauddin, pro-vice chancellor at the time.[11] The university court was scheduled to meet on 15 April 1928, but Dr Ziauddin resigned as pro-VC on 26 March 1928. Dr Ziauddin's resignation was accepted in a special meeting of the executive council on 30 March 1928. Meanwhile, Nawab Muzamillullah Khan was the acting vice chancellor after the resignation of

Sahabzada Aftab Ahmad Khan as VC on 31 December 1926. Ross Masood would take charge as VC on 29 October 1929. But let us see briefly what he did in England.

Theodore Morison, the third principal of MAO College, who officiated between 1899 and 1904, had returned to England. It was to his care that Ross Masood had been entrusted after Morison had discovered that the young boy was put to work in the fields that cold, dark night in the 1890s. In England too, Morison and his wife were Ross's local guardians. It was through the Morisons that Ross Masood was introduced to Edward Morgan Forster, who later became a famous novelist. Masood needed a tutor to learn Latin from. Morison's wife knew someone whose son (E.M. Forster) had graduated from Cambridge, where he had studied Latin and Greek. In November 1906, E.M. Forster became a Latin tutor to Ross Masood. It developed into a lifelong friendship. When Forster visited India for the first time in 1912, Masood accompanied him to many places in the country. Forster dedicated his landmark novel *A Passage to India* to Ross Masood. Significantly, Masood didn't forget India and Aligarh while in England. He wrote a letter titled 'How should the Aligarh Muslim University be', which was published by Muhammad Ali in his Delhi-based newspaper *The Comrade*.[12]

It was to resuscitate the lost glory of AMU, to inject a new life into the creaking body of the university, that Ross Masood agreed to become its vice chancellor on 20 October 1929. Strachey Hall, which had hosted Ross Masood's Bismillah in 1893 and his farewell on the eve of his departure to England in 1906, was hosting him again.

Jalil Qidwai, a fawning admirer of Ross Masood who later established the Ross Masood Educational and Cultural Society in Karachi, has captured the mood when Ross Masood entered the historic Strachey Hall in purple Urdu prose. Qidwai writes: A red-whitish, tall and huge man wearing smart English dress, his face radiant with steely determination, entered the hall amidst loud applause. Without waiting for a moment, he went straight to dais and began speaking.[13]

If he had a dream, a design for AMU, Ross Masood declared it publicly in that very first address as the institution's head. It deserves to be quoted in some detail:

> Today I am addressing you from a place from where the founder of this institution would send out his message to the people of his times. He is the man whose blood is running in my veins and who lies buried a few steps away from here ... I am not the one who ... (quashes) the empty dreams of the youth ... I have always sympathized with the aspirations of the youth ... I refuse to accept that Muslims as a community are dead. And I believe that the youth of a living community cannot create a new world without dazzling dreams and rosy aspirations ... Let me make it clear to you all that till the day the university's reign is in my hands, nothing second grade will be accepted. I want to see everything first grade here.[14]

That was both a clarion call and declaration of the roadmap. And Ross Masood set out to make changes in right earnest. He wanted to make the necessary changes in the administration and create a team that was professional and loyal. He brought in a pro-vice chancellor and a registrar of his choice. Having created new posts and filled empty ones, Ross Masood focused on the teaching of science. He embarked on the ambitious project of attracting the best brains from India and abroad. He wrote to the famous scientist Albert Einstein to recommend a teacher for physics. Einstein sent Dr Rudolph Samuel, one of his proteges and an expert in spectroscopy. 'Prominent European scientist Prof. R.F. Hunter was appointed in the department of chemistry'[15]. Journalist Tariq Hasan describes this era as the golden period of the university:

'Such was the promise of AMU in those days that Arnold Toynbee, one of the greatest historians in his era, recommended the name of William Hass for appointment in the Department of History. Eminent Indian scholars from different spheres of studies like noted scientist Sir C.V. Raman, Sir Jadunath Sarkar, Sir Mohammad Iqbal and Dr Tara Chand were prominent among those who were invited to deliver lectures on the campus. It was during this period that Aligarh sought to create a very special niche for itself as the focal point for the emergence of a revitalized forward looking, modern, resurgent Islam.'[16]

If his grandfather had modelled MAO College on the lines of Oxford, Ross Masood wanted Aligarh to be truly be Oxford of the East. These days it is very rare that a vice chancellor gives classes and lectures. But Ross Masood gave lectures on the education system in Japan at the Students' Union Hall. Dr Abid Hussain, a friend of Dr Zakir Hussain's, once observed: 'At the time Ross Masood came to Aligarh Muslim University, it looked like a city of the dead. He brought remarkable and visible changes in academic life, literary and cultural societies and in the gymnastics and sporting fields. Every walk of life of the students and teachers saw a new vigour.'[17] Before Ross Masood became its VC, a design for the science faculty building had already been made, but Masood rejected the design, saying: 'I don't want to build stable-like buildings to house science faculties.'

Also, before Ross became the VC, the university had been perpetually deficient in funds. Through his efforts, the government released a one-time grant of Rs 15 lakh and increased the annual grant from Rs 1.25 lakh to Rs 3 lakh. The Nizam of Hyderabad gave a donation of Rs 10 lakh and increased his annual grant from Rs 36,000 to Rs 60,000. Maulvi Abdul Haq wrote: 'He (Ross Masood) brought in so much money to the University that no one had imagined even in their dreams.'[18]

Since he wanted AMU to excel in science teaching, Masood put his efforts into creating the infrastructure for this. He got buildings constructed for the departments of chemistry, botany and zoology. He was passionately involved in making Aligarh a centre for science teaching. In a letter to a friend on 25 May 1932, he wrote: 'You will be happy to know that, by God's grace, our new science laboratory is completing shortly. This will be considered a fine laboratory in India. I want this university [to be] the biggest centre in the world for learning science for Muslims.'[19] He also oversaw the construction of some of the residential hostels for students, including Aftab Hall and Viqarul Mulk (VM) Hall. Sultan Jahan Begum funded the construction of Nasrullah Hostel, named after her son who had died young.

Ross didn't believe in frugal living and never romanticized poverty. 'I cannot give education to students while they are in a loincloth like Gandhi or seated under a tree like Tagore,' he would often say.[20] The science faculty buildings that came up in his period were the best among the universities in the India of that era. Ross also promoted the teaching of agricultural science in the university.

A connoisseur of the arts, poetry and painting, Ross Masood made AMU culturally vibrant. He had memorized hundreds of couplets in Urdu, Persian and English and could quote them at the drop of a hat. A big mushaira was also held at the university during his term.

Since the Muslim League sympathizers on the campus had begun asserting themselves due to the changing political situation in the country, it was not easy to invite prominent national leaders there. However, Masood showed maturity and did some sort of balancing act. Remember, it was still British India and the Raj would not be very happy to see leaders of India's freedom struggle getting a great reception at a government-funded campus.

Though he never took part in active politics, Ross Masood was politically astute. Since the Muslim League was getting its foothold in the university, inviting nationalist leaders to the university as guests was risky. The university administration avoided inviting leaders like Mahatma Gandhi and Jawaharlal Nehru. On 4 November 1929, the group of nationalist students at AMU invited Gandhiji without discussing it with the vice chancellor or any other member of the administration. However, Ross Masood attended the function and accorded a warm welcome to Gandhiji.

Prominent among the nationalist students in that period were Khwaja Ahmed Abbas, Akhtar Raipuri and Hayatullah Ansari. While Raipuri and Ansari became famous Urdu writers and journalists, Abbas went on to make a name as a columnist, film writer and director in Mumbai (then Bombay). Jawaharlal Nehru was the hero of the left-leaning nationalist students like Khwaja Ahmed Abbas. Again, without informing Ross Masood, the nationalist boys invited Nehru. The historian Prof Habib had sent an introductory letter to Nehru, who agreed to attend their function at the Union Club. However, when Ross Masood heard about this, he told the students that instead of felicitating Nehru at the Union Club, he would be hosted at Strachey Hall as it would be a university function. Masood and Nehru were family friends. Masood took Nehru to Strachey Hall and, introducing him to the audience, he said: 'My sons and friends, I am introducing you to my big friend Motilal Nehru's elder son Jawaharlal Nehru.'[21] This calmed nerves all around. After delivering his speech, Nehru returned to Delhi the same day.

In 1928, only a year before Ross Masood had joined AMU as its VC, he had divorced his wife Sahabzadi Zohra Begum, the only daughter of Sahabzada Aftab Ahmad Khan, a student of MAO College and a former VC. Their wedding in 1914 was a big event in Aligarh, with students of MAO College, many old boys, and eminent citizens of Aligarh and elsewhere participating in the celebrations. The Ali brothers (Muhammad Ali and Shaukat Ali) were so enthused that as the horse-drawn carriage left Mahmood Manzil or Peeli Kothi (Ross Masood's mother Begum Mahmood's residence near Sir Syed Hall) for Aftab Manzil near Shamshad Market in Aligarh, the Ali brothers untied the horse and themselves pulled the carriage to the doorstep of Aftab Manzil. Many thousand guests enjoyed the multi-course feast served by the family of Sahabzada Aftab Ahmad Khan, who was the Nawab of Karnal. Four days later, on 18 November, a lavish reception was held at the sprawling lawns of Sir Syed House. The host was Begum Mahmood, who had brought up her only son Ross with great care and love. Her relationship with Masood's father Syed Mahmood had soured because of his heavy drinking and irascible temper. Syed Mahmood had moved to Sitapur in 1901 to live with his cousin Syed Mohammed Ahmed. He died there in 1903 and was buried beside his father at the Jama Masjid courtyard in the college campus. After a long time, happiness had returned to Begum Mahmood's house, and she left no stone unturned to mark it with gaiety.

Ross Masood didn't believe in groupism. Unlike his many predecessors and successors, he didn't create any camp. Neither did he belong to any camp. He wanted to put AMU on the path of progress. He tried his best and succeeded too, to a great extent. But then, every good thing has to come to an end. Another term might have given him the opportunity to take the university to greater heights, but he resigned on 30 September 1934, and Dr Ziauddin succeeded him as VC. The news of Ross Masood's resignation as VC was a big blow to well-wishers of the university. Both the Nawab of Bhopal, Hamidullah Khan, who had become chancellor of AMU, and the poet Allama Iqbal tried to persuade Ross Masood to withdraw his resignation, but he had made up his mind. Actually, Ross Masood had wanted an extension of the registrar Fakhruddin Ahmed's tenure, but Dr Ziauddin and his supporters were opposed to it. Ziauddin's group had threatened that if the VC used the power of the executive council to give an extension to the registrar, it would be defeated in the university court. Ziauddin's group was in a majority at the court, and Ross Masood saw this threat as a referendum on his term as vice chancellor and decided to resign. Nawab Hamidullah Khan too resigned as chancellor after a few months of Ross Masood's resignation.

Ross Masood had stayed at the Sir Syed House while he was vice chancellor. He was emotionally attached to this house as he was born in one of its rooms and had spent his childhood here. The old charm of the place in the days gone by, when Sir Syed would host his friends there, seemed to have returned to it.

Ross Masood had two sons—Anwar Masood and Akbar Masood—from his first wife Zohra Begum. After his divorce from his first wife Zohra Begum, Ross Masood married Umtul Rashid Begum in 1933, while he was still VC of AMU. She was reverentially called Lady Masood. Daughter of Ross Masood's classmate at Aligarh and Oxford, Mohammed Abdur Rashid Khan, Lady Masood was highly educated and knew several languages, including Urdu, Persian, English and French. They had first met at a common friend's house in Shimla and had liked each other.

Soon after quitting the VC's post, Masood received an offer from the princely state of Bhopal to be the education minister there. But before moving to Bhopal, Masood and Lady Masood went on a brief vacation to London. The couple's stay in Bhopal for three years (1934–1937) was pleasant and happy. They were accommodated at Reyaz Manzil, the beautiful mansion on the bank of Bhopal's biggest lake. The ground floor was the office, and it also had a dining room; the delightfully decorated living rooms were on the upper floor. Allama Iqbal, a great friend of Ross Masood, would stay in one of these rooms on his visits to Bhopal from Lahore. 'Between 1935 and 1936, Iqbal came to Bhopal thrice for treatment at the request of Ross Masood.'[22] It is because of Ross Masood that Iqbal's bond with the Bhopal state cemented, though Iqbal and Nawab Hamidullah Khan had known each other for decades. On his second visit to Bhopal, Iqbal stayed at Sheesh Mahal, the nawab's palace, as a state guest. His stay there gave the great poet some much-needed comfort that enabled him to produce some of his best verse. Iqbal's son Javed Iqbal had accompanied him on this visit. 'My father and I would have dinner at Reyaz Manzil once or twice a week. Once when we were returning from there, there was a middle-aged, heavily built lady in our car. My father later told me that she was Sarojini Naidu,' recalled Javed Iqbal.[23]

Ross Masood and Lady Masood had a daughter. On Iqbal's suggestion, she was named Nadira. On Ross Masood's request, the Nawab of Bhopal granted a monthly stipend of Rs 500 to Iqbal, who was in dire straits financially at the time. Even Sir Aga Khan, on Masood's request, had granted a monthly stipend of Rs 500 to Iqbal, but the poet refused to accept, it saying that the monthly stipend of Rs 500 from Bhopal state would suffice.

Ross Masood suffered from kidney disease and suffered bouts of shooting pain in the abdomen. In May 1937 he fell seriously ill. He had returned from Europe without completing his treatment for the disease. He had fallen ill in 1927 too, but had recovered after treatment in Germany. But this time, despite the efforts of some of the best doctors, he couldn't recover. He passed away on 30 July 1937. He was only forty-eight. Nawab Hamidullah Khan was travelling in England at the time, but his high officials made all the arrangements for Ross Masood's burial at the royal graveyard in Bhopal. However, Ross Masood's mother Musharraf Jahan Begum, aka Begum Mahmood, sent a telegram asking for his body to be sent to Aligarh. The next day his body travelled by a first-class train compartment to Agra station, where Masood's first wife Zohra

Begum too had arrived, to accompany the body in a lorry to his mother's house in Aligarh.

A huge crowd had assembled there to say goodbye to the only grandson of Sir Syed, the old man of Aligarh who had brought a renaissance in the life of the subcontinent's Muslims. The funeral procession reached the cricket ground, and after the namaz-e-janaza, Ross Masood was buried near his grandfather's grave. Grandfather and grandson—the old man and the child on whom he had doted a lot—rest peacefully close to each other. The poet Iqbal, who had written a quatrain in Persian for his own tombstone, sent it to be inscribed on Ross Masood's tombstone. It loosely translates as:

> I didn't lose my heart to this world
> Because I am free from restrictions big and small
> When I saw the morning breeze briefly
> The flowers had gone after showing their colours and
> brightness

Thus ended the journey of a remarkable man, the true inheritor of Sir Syed's legacy.

4

After the Storm: Two Stalwarts Who Saved AMU

FOR great men, the welfare of people and institutions comes before their personal likes and dislikes. They also swallow humiliations and forgive others' misdemeanours towards them. In the earlier chapters we saw how Maulana Abul Kalam Azad was humiliated by AMU students, and how, but for the good sense of his co-passengers on the Kalka Express who shut the compartment from inside, he might have been lynched by the students at Aligarh railway station. That day in 1945, Maulana Azad had even tried to come out of the compartment and face the mob of students, but his fellow passengers had held him back. Sweating profusely, the usually well-dressed Maulana looked distraught, his sherwani torn and crumpled. Anyone in his place would have harboured antipathy towards a university

64

whose students had humiliated him publicly. But Maulana Azad was neither mean-minded nor vengeful towards AMU or the AMU community.

That the Maulana had forgiven the Aligarh students for the indignity to which they had subjected him was evident when he, as the education minister, in consultation with Prime Minister Jawaharlal Nehru, chose Dr Zakir Hussain to take command of AMU after the holocaust of Partition. Partition and the communal rage in its aftermath had nearly killed AMU.

Maulana Azad's trust in Aligarh ran so deep that after the Anjuman Taraqqi Urdu secretary, Dr Abdul Haq, migrated to Pakistan (we have discussed his role at the Darul Tarjuma or Translation Bureau in Hyderabad state), Azad had the Anujman shifted to Aligarh. Eminent Urdu writer Qazi Abdul Ghaffar was made its secretary. The Anjuman later shifted to Delhi. Maulana Azad's bonds with AMU further strengthened when a group of young scholars, great devotees of his, established Azad Academy in Aligarh to propagate his ideas. This academic-cum-literary body held discussions on his political and social ideas. One of the founders of this Azad Academy was Riaz-ur-Rahman Sherwani, grandson of Sadar Yar Jung Habibur Rahman Khan Sherwani and son of Ubaidur Rahman Khan Sherwani, who was twice treasurer at AMU. Riaz-ur-Rahman had been in Shimla with his brother and sister when Partition happened. They had crossed over to Pakistan because returning to Aligarh would have been risky as the riots had begun. However, Riaz-ur-Rahman got disenchanted with the new country, and after two years there returned to Aligarh, where he taught Arabic. In an interview to Eram Agha of *The Times of India* in 2016, he had recalled: 'The (Pakistan) government gave us a place to stay because my family back here (Aligarh) was influential, but

I didn't want to stay in a country which was dominated by a single religious identity. I wanted to come back to the plurality of India.' He returned to India in 1949. The Sherwanis have an illustrious history and a great relationship with AMU. Apart from being impressed with Maulana Azad's scholarship, Riaz-ur-Rahman had another reason for his great love for Maulana Azad. Here is why.

Maulana Azad was sent to prison in Ahmednagar for three years (1942–1945). While in jail, he wrote letters to Sadar Yar Jung Habibur Rahman Khan Sherwani, the Nawab of Bhikampur, near Aligarh. The letters were never posted. After his release from jail, he published these letters in a book, *Ghubar-e-Khatir*, a masterpiece of Urdu literature. Who was this Habibur Rahman Khan Sherwani, to whom Maulana Azad wrote letters from prison?

Belonging to the nawab family of Bhikampur, Habibur Rahman Khan's father Mohammed Taqi Khan built a citadel adjacent to Bhikampur for his son and named it Habib Ganj. The citadel or garhi in Urdu had a beautiful garden and opulent mansions. Unlike scions of many contemporary Maharajas, Rajas and Nawabs who kept harems where beauties abounded and also kept stables where horses of Arab breed received royal treatment, Habibur Rahman Khan had lost his heart to books. He loved reading and writing, prolifically penned prose and poetry and created a rich library that stocked many rare books and manuscripts. His reputation as a patron of arts, scholars and scholarship spread far and wide. He also headed AMU's Theology department and the seventh Nizam of Hyderabad,

Mir Osman Ali Khan, appointed him head of religious affairs of the Hyderabad State. He became even first Vice-Chancellor of Osmania University on its founding in 1919. Acknowledging his love for letters and services, Mir Osman Ali conferred the title of 'Sadar Yar Jung Bahadur' on him. Habibur Rahman returned to Habib Ganj in 1930 and got himself associated with several educational institutions and remained engaged in seeking and spreading knowledge till his death in 1950.[1]

Habibur Rahman's family donated his rare books, manuscripts and artifacts to AMU, which are displayed in the Habib Ganj Collection section at the Maulana Azad Library. Pakistani writer-civil servant Mukhtar Masood draws an interesting comparison between Jinnah's frequent visits to Aligarh in the 1940s and Maulana Azad's letters to Habibur Rahman Khan Sherwani. In Aligarh, Jinnah would stay at Habib Manzil, Habirbur Rahman Khan's bungalow. Masood writes:

> Those days when Quaid-i-Azam used to stay here (at Habib Manzil), a prisoner at Ahmednagar wrote letters to him (Sherwani) and kept them. These letters were published post-release of the prisoner (Maulana Azad) in a collection called Ghubar-e-Khatir. And, courtesy the prose of Abul Kalam Azad, the noble of Bhikampur entered the history of Urdu literature.[2]

So, Maulana Azad's choice of Dr Zakir Hussain as VC for AMU after Partition was well thought out. Those who blame AMU for overwhelmingly supporting the demand for Pakistan forget that around 40 per cent of the teachers and students came from areas (Punjab, Sindh and Baluchistan) that went to Pakistan. A number of Muslim League supporters sought greener pastures and went to Pakistan, abandoning the beautiful campus Sir Syed had created, a campus to which a poet like Asrarul Haq Majaz, an alumnus, composed a eulogy '*Yeh mera chaman hai ...*' (this is my garden). This poem became the university tarana or anthem and is recited with great gusto at all festive occasions at the institution. Majaz was immensely popular among the girls on the campus. While he was studying at Aligarh, the girls in the women's college would recite his romantic poems and hold a qurra andazi (lottery) of their names to find out who would marry Majaz. Years later Majaz met writer Athar Parvez at Allahabad station. They began talking about an essay the famous short-story writer Ismat Chughtai had written about her Aligarh days:

Majaz to Parvez: '*Are mian, is almiya par nazar nahin padi ke mere naam Womens' College ki ladkiyan qurrey dala karti thi aur suno Ismat bhi un qurron mein shareek hoti thi ... Lekin tragedy yeh hai ke ek taraf to hamare naam ke qurray padte the aur doosri taraf hum ladkiyon ki shakal dekhne ko taraste the. Yeh ladkiyan waqai zalim hoti hain. Ishq hum se karti hai aur shadi Shahid Latif se*' (Dear friend, didn't you see the irony, that girls at the women's college would put their names in a lottery to marry me and even Ismat [Chughtai] was among them. But the tragedy is that while they did a lottery to marry me, I was longing to see the faces of the girls. These girls really tormented me. They love me but marry Shahid Latif).

Ismat Chughtai had married filmmaker Shahid Latif.

Why did Majaz say that he longed to see the faces of the women students at AMU? Women's education at Aligarh was introduced much after MAO College was started in 1877. Rahat Abrar, in his book *Muslim Taaleeem-e-Niswan ke Sau Saal: Chilman se Chand Tak* (Hundred years of Muslim Women's Education: From Purdah to the Moon), maps the journey of Muslim women's education at Aligarh. Shaikh Abdullah, who was among the first generation of MAO College students, wanted to begin a school for girls, but he was not allowed to start one on the MAO College campus. 'Even the British principal Archbold saw a school for girls on the campus as harmful for the health of the College.'[3] Abdullah started this school in 1906 at the Tantan Para area at the Upper Court, 5 km from the campus. Later it was shifted to Marris Road and became Abdullah Girls' College, a leading institution for Muslim women's education in the subcontinent. Since there were not many female teachers available, male teachers were roped in to teach, but there was a chilman or purdah suspended between the male teacher and the women students. Discouragement to women's education also came from satirists like the poet Akbar Allahabadi (1846–1921), who mocked the idea in couplets such as this one: '*Ilm-e-maghrib padh ke hongi aisi khudsar bibiyan/ Bibiyan shauhar banengi aur shuhar bibiyan* (Having studied the knowledge of the west, the wives will be so headstrong/ [That] wives will become husbands and husbands, wives).'[4]

Later, for MA classes, co-education was introduced, where both boys and girls sat in classrooms without a chilmun or curtain drawn between them. Farrukh Waris, who joined AMU in 1971 for her post-graduate course in history, recalls that the girls at AMU never felt subjugated. 'My friend Fatima Bilgrami wore a burqa, but mentally she was and is so liberated that when I told her to get her ears pierced for earrings, she dismissed it as a sign of slavery. Aligarh opened our minds and empowered us to see the world from a fresh perspective. The girls there may not wear bikinis, but are mentally liberated,' says Waris. However, undergraduate girl students were not allowed to sit in the Maulana Azad Library, the university's central library, till a few years ago. We will examine that in detail in the coming chapters.

More than establishing gender equality at AMU, Zakir Hussain's bigger concern was to establish stability there. He wanted to gain the confidence of both the nationalists and those who had been pro-Muslim League before Partition, because many of the latter category had stayed back, reposing their faith in India. For Zakir Hussain it was a sweet irony, as he was among those who had rebelled against AMU's pro-government approach in 1920 and had left it, founding Jamia Millia in the vicinity of the MAO College they were so proud of. Zakir Hussain and Muhammad Ali were among the rebels forcefully evicted from their hostel rooms by the police who had been called in by MAO College Principal Sir Ziauddin. How much Dr Zakir Hussain loved AMU can be gauged from a speech he delivered on 11 August 1952 at Sir Syed Hall:

> I always feel happy when I come to Aligarh. When I was a student, I looked upon Aligarh as my all. It was my home, my garden, my native land. If for any reason I parted from Aligarh even for a short time, my heart was filled with thoughts of this home, this garden, this native land ... (But) even while I was a student, I was cut away from Aligarh. I and some of my friends had

rebelled against this institution. The authorities were not willing to let it become what we wanted it to become, to agree with what we considered to be its real purpose ... The police came, put me in a truck and took me to the railway station. My coming here was forbidden. After this, I and my colleagues began working in the Jamia. We had founded the Jamia Millia after rebelling against this place, but we never regarded the Jamia as something apart. I worked wholeheartedly in the Jamia Millia for 27 years because I felt that there, too, I was working for Aligarh. I was convinced that one day we would return to Aligarh and make it the focus of our hopes and dreams ... [5]

In 1925, Jamia Millia was moved to Karol Bagh in Delhi, where it ran from a few rooms. After completing his PhD from Germany, Zakir Hussain and two other friends, Abid Hussain and Mohammed Mujeeb, returned to teach at Jamia. Zakir Hussain became Jamia's Shaikhul Jamia or vice chancellor and gave his sweat and blood to it, nurturing it for twenty-seven years.

Heading AMU was a challenge for Zakir Hussain. He could make or mar its destiny. Though the majority of League supporters at AMU had left for Pakistan, there was a section that had stayed back and viewed Zakir Hussain with suspicion. 'A section of the students looked upon Zakir Hussain as an intruder, even as one foisted by a government which, it was said, saw AMU as polluted because of its pro-Pakistan past and wished to "purify" it.'[6]

Since a section of Indians saw Muslims and AMU with suspicion and held them responsible for the division of India, the staunch nationalist and patriot Zakir Hussain set about allaying the fears of the community. Along with Maulana Azad, he led from the front and defended the community which had chosen to make India their home. M. Mujeeb tells us that at the end of 1948 there were only three professors—including Prof. Babur Mirza, who taught zoology—who had actively backed the Muslim League.

> Among the junior staff members and the students there were not many who had remained unaffected by the communal epidemic. Dr Zakir Hussain's first task was to allay fear and suspicion. It became apparent very soon that he was a man of goodwill to whose nature anything that smacked of vindictiveness or brainwashing was completely foreign. This created a feeling of confidence which was the starting point in the rehabilitation of the Muslim University.[7]

Addressing the 1951 convocation at AMU, headed by then President Dr Rajendra Prasad, Zakir Hussain said:

> The general Indian public, the Indian press, insufficiently informed Indian public men are only too ready to accept anything bad about us. I can understand this readiness but as an Indian I feel I must do everything to see that this unhealthy attitude does not make loyal Muslim Indian citizens feel that they can be looked upon as foreigners in their own country ... [8]

He injected a sense of confidence among both teachers and students, especially those who had sided with the Pakistan movement but had chosen to stay back. In a sense, Zakir Hussain tried to get Indian Muslims to repose their faith in Indian secularism, its democratic principles and pluralistic ethos. He kept his doors open for all, creating a congenial atmosphere. It was said that if students went to see him with their sherwanis unbuttoned down to the waist, the VC would button up their long coats while talking to them.

One of his rehabilitation plans for AMU was to hire fresh blood and pick up professors, readers and lecturers from other universities. Dr Zakir Hussain would often meet post-graduate students individually, helping many to study abroad. Many years after he left AMU, there were still several teachers in senior positions whom he had helped in one way or the other.

A lasting contribution Dr Zakir Hussain made to Aligarh was turning it into a green campus. A nature lover, he got planted beautiful bougainvillea and other flowering plants and trees on both sides of the university roads. Gardening was his hobby.

Zakir Hussain had agreed to take charge as AMU vice chancellor on one condition: he wanted to be elected by the university court and not appointed as the government nominee. Acting vice chancellor Nawab Mohammad Ismail Khan resigned on 28 November 1948, and two days later Zakir Hussain took charge at the helm of AMU.

The Aligarh Muslim University (Amendment) Act, 1951, the first amendment since 1920, introduced a couple of major changes. The VC's term was now fixed for six years instead of three. Zakir Hussain got an extension of three years, though he resigned in 1956, a year before his term was about to end. This Act also made religious study optional, as under the

Constitution of India, institutions that received government funding couldn't make religious study compulsory. The act attracted the displeasure of some Muslims also because it allowed, for the first time, non-Muslims to be elected to the university court. In fact, the reforms in the rules governing AMU and Banaras Hindu University (BHU) were brought in around the same time. Membership of the court at AMU had been restricted to Muslims, and membership of the university court at BHU was restricted to Hindus. The Banaras Hindu University (Amendment) Act, 1951, too opened court membership to non-Hindus. Zakir Hussain wanted BHU and AMU to retain their characteristics but also become more inclusive. To him, the teaching of Islamic religion and theology at AMU or the focus on Vedic, Hindu, Buddhist and Jain studies at BHU did not in any way contradict the spirit of the country's secular Constitution. He said: 'A secular republic will have a Hindu university and a Muslim university as central universities because only a secular republic has the large-heartedness, the tolerance to have them both.'[9]

Secular to the core, Zakir Hussain, following the new act, stressed that the university would follow the country's secular Constitution. When Zakir Hussain reduced the annual leave for Muharram, student leader Jaffer Mehdi Tabaan sat on a hunger strike. To show solidarity with his demand, the students' union held a meeting which even the VC attended. Another student leader, Ahmed Saeed, whom the students had nicknamed Anda (Eggs), used a pun on Zakir Hussain's first name in his speech and said: *'Afsoos hai ke is Jamia mein Zakir Hussain Zikre Hussain ko mana karta hai'* (It is regrettable that in this university Zakir Hussain is stopping students from mourning martyrdom of Hussain).[10]

Zakir Hussain invited Maulana Azad, the education minister, to deliver the annual convocation address on 20 February 1949. Zakir Hussain rightly hoped that his speech would mark a turning point in the life of Indian Muslims. Azad, a powerful orator and essayist in Urdu, didn't disappoint his host when he said:

You belong to an institution which led the Muslim renaissance in the nineteenth century. Unfortunately, after the passing away of its founder Sir Syed Ahmad Khan, the movement which he led could not fully live up to its expectations. I want to assure you that if you have to imbibe the spirit of the founding fathers, if you show real strength of character and if you work hard to make this place a centre of excellence in the field of education then no one can stop you from reaping the harvest of your efforts.[11]

Maulana Azad had the ability to weave words into clarion calls. He admitted to have been hugely influenced by Sir Syed's writings and devouring almost every word that Sir Syed wrote. He was aware of the historic importance of the work Sir Syed and his close associates had done at MAO College. Paying tribute to Sir Syed, Maulana Azad, in the same address, said: 'Sir Syed had established in Aligarh not only a college but an intellectual and cultural centre in tune with the progressive spirit of the times. The centre of this circle was Sir Syed himself and he attracted around him some of the best intellectuals of the day.'[12]

The 'intellectuals' that Maulana Azad spoke of comprised the Urdu poet, critic and biographer of Sir Syed, Altaf Hussain

Hali, poet-teacher and Islamic scholar Shibli Nomani, associates like Mohsinul Mulk and Viqarul Mulk, fiction writer Nazir Ahmed, MAO College Principal Theodore Beck and Orientalist Professor T.W. Arnold.

Arnold, a Cambridge graduate, was appointed professor of philosophy in 1887 on Beck's recommendation. Changing into the Oriental dress of churidar, turban and angarkha, Arnold had the delightful task of doing the head count at the mosque during the prayers. He chided the absentees gently. He adopted Oriental ways to such an extent that Sir Syed and many others on the campus called him 'Maulana Arnold'. In 1889, the poet Hali captured the portrait of Arnold in a couplet:

'*Maseehi poshishen dekhein Musalmanon ke bachon ki/ Maseehi ko Musalmani quba zeb-e-badan dekhein* (You may see Muslim boys at the college wearing Christian or western dress and a Christian in Muslim dress).'[13]

Arnold even organized iftar parties for a select group of college students and teachers at his residence. He resigned in 1897 to become the principal of Oriental College, Lahore, where he mentored Iqbal, who went on to become a celebrated poet, well known as Allama Sir Mohammad Iqbal.

Azad wanted to save that sanctuary, that intellectual hub, from getting blown away in the storm in the aftermath of Partition. And speaking of his oratorial skills, mention must be made of the speech he delivered in Delhi soon after Partition. On 23 October 1947, Maulana Azad reached the stone steps of the Mughal-era Jama Masjid to deliver one of most soul-stirring speeches in modern Indian history. Enticed by the promise of a new land that leaders of Muslim League, especially Jinnah, had dangled before them, many Muslims in Delhi were planning to leave for Pakistan. Mixing history, metaphor and

Quranic injunctions, and listing the instances of deceit by the Muslim League of the subcontinent's Muslims, Maulana Azad told the gathering to eschew escapism and stay back in India. The speech deserves to be quoted in detail:

Do you remember? I hailed you, you cut off my tongue; I picked my pen, you severed my hand; I wanted to move forward, you broke off my legs; I tried to run, and you injured my back. When the bitter political games of the last seven years were at their peak, I tried to wake you up at every danger signal. You not only ignored my call but revived all the past traditions of neglect and denial. As a result, the same perils surround you today, whose onset had previously diverted you from the righteous path ... It was not long ago when I warned you that the two-nation theory was death knell to a meaningful, dignified life; forsake it. I told you that the pillars upon which you were leaning would inevitably crumble. To all this you turned a deaf ear. You did not realize that, my brothers! I have always attempted to keep politics apart from personalities, thus avoiding those thorny valleys. That is why some of my messages are often couched in allusions. The Partition of India was a fundamental mistake. The manner in which religious differences were incited, inevitably, led to the devastation that we have seen with our own eyes. Unfortunately, we are still seeing it at some places ... Where are you going and why? Raise your eyes. The minarets of Jama Masjid want to ask you a question. Where have you lost the glorious pages from your chronicles? Was it only yesterday that on the banks of the Jamuna, your caravans performed

wazu? Today, you are afraid of living here. Remember,
Delhi has been nurtured with your blood. Brothers,
create a basic change in yourselves. Today, your fear is
misplaced as your jubilation was yesterday.[14]

After the 1949 convocation, in the evening the students' union
invited Maulana Azad for a reception. It was part of the same
tradition following which the students' union would invite
former Vice President Hamid Ansari to the Union Club for a
reception years later. The uproar over Jinnah's portrait and the
violence had forced the cancellation of Ansari's reception and
his address. While forces outside the university had created a
ruckus that led to violence and cancellation of Ansari's address,
it was an AMU student and an office-bearer of the students'
union who made uncomplimentary remarks about Maulana
Azad's convocation address. Students' union Vice President
Shah Hasan Ata made some uncharitable remarks about
Maulana Azad's convocation address. It hurt Azad so much
that he vowed never to return to Aligarh. Azad kept his word.

AMU apologized for the hurt caused to Maulana Azad
by naming its central library after him. One of the biggest
repositories on Indo-Mughal history, the library currently
has thirteen lakh books. In 2017, in a gesture of generosity,
Maulana Azad's legal heirs donated some of his personal
belongings, watches, pens, a dinner set and his commentary on
the Quran to the Maulana Azad library. All these belongings are
displayed there. Acknowledging the institution's indebtedness
to the legal heirs of Maulana Azad, then AMU vice chancellor
Zameeruddin Shah said: 'Post-Independence, there were some
hostile sentiments against AMU. He (Maulana Azad) had

helped to preserve the university's character. We were delighted and honoured to have this collection bequeathed to us.'[15]

Zakir Hussain managed to rescue AMU. He provided the salve for its healing at a time when it faced an existential crisis. He mended many fault lines in the university, but factionalism on the campus raised its ugly head again. Rajmohan Gandhi observes:

> Not everyone at AMU praised Zakir Hussain. Some of the meetings he had to conduct were unpleasant. There were insinuations that he had created a 'new' Aligarh of the sort desired by New Delhi. Giving in to his unhappiness, Zakir Hussain once said publicly that he had lost hope of anything worthwhile being done at AMU. To the middle of 1956, a year before his turn was to end, he resigned.[16]

But the fact remains that the two stalwarts, Maulana Azad and Dr Zakir Hussain, saved AMU. But for them, the dream of Sir Syed would have ended in the holocaust of Partition.

5

A Modern Institution or Madrassa?

IF you walk down the tree-lined road from Bab-e-Syed at AMU's southern periphery to Centenary Gate on the university's northern boundary, you may bump into many young sherwani-clad bearded men. It is not that the sherwani or beard is a new fashion fad on the campus. They have always been there. In fact, sherwani and the Aligarh-cut white churidar for men have been a sort of uniform for formal occasions for ages here. But in some quarters, the opinion is that they are more visible because of an increasing number of madrassa students joining courses at AMU. Many first-time visitors may mistake the campus for an advanced madrassa. Maulvis who have already acquired some learning in the Islamic religious texts enter the mainstream secular courses courtesy a provision in the Aligarh Muslim University (Amendment) Act, 1981.

Section 5(2)C of the Act mandates the university to 'promote educational and cultural advancement of Muslims in India'.[1] A committee headed by a former pro-VC, Prof. Mohammed Shafi, was set up in 1986 to recommend steps for implementation of this section. Among other things, the Shafi Committee suggested that a centre be established to carry out the mandate in the Act. The Centre for Promotion of Educational and Cultural Advancement of the Muslims of India (CPECAMI) was thus established in 1988. It was under the same Section 5(2)C that the Centre for Promotion of Science was established in 1985. Its primary objective was to create awareness among Muslims about the need to acquire scientific knowledge and promote science education in Muslim-managed educational institutions, including madrassas. So, how did AMU, a modern institution over which founder Sir Syed had faced strong opposition from the maulvis in the last quarter of nineteenth century, become a magnet for madrassa-educated students? Many on the campus hold two former vice chancellors— Saiyid Hamid and Lt. General (Retired) Zameer Uddin Shah— responsible for opening AMU's gates wide for the maulvis.

Saiyid Hamid was an AMU alumnus and a retired civil servant. His term as VC (1980–1985) saw huge protests by students, one of whom was even killed in police firing at a demonstration. But Hamid introduced many changes too. Farrukh Waris, an AMU alumnus and family friend of Saiyid Hamid, remembers an interesting anecdote about him. She says that when the campaign against Saiyid Hamid became virulent and he too grew impatient and wanted to resign, he contacted then Prime Minister Indira Gandhi.[2] Farrukh Waris says:

'Indira Gandhi told Saiyid Hamid that *ek Syed ne AMU qayam kiya aur doosre Syed ko AMU ko bachana hai* (One Syed, that is Sir Syed, founded AMU and another Syed, or Saiyid Hamid, had to save it). And Saiyid Hamid left no stone unturned to not only rescue the university from going to the dogs, he also enhanced its stature.'

Ishtiaq Ali was an MA student when the agitation against Saiyid Hamid was at its peak. He was the convener of the Students' Academic Forum, a platform created to support Saiyid Hamid while the students' union was opposing him. Ishtiaq Ali says that several senior students had been occupying the hostel rooms for years and would not vacate them even as the newcomers were facing difficulty in getting accommodation. This problem had become acute during the time of Saiyid Hamid's predecessor, the economist A.M. Khusro, who allowed laxity in admissions and other irregularities. Sunil Sethi, then correspondent of *India Today*, had visited the AMU campus in February 1981 to report on the turmoil that was happening. He found that an interview given by the eminent historian Prof. Irfan Habib, who was dean of the faculty of social sciences, had further stirred the agitators. Sethi reported:

Ostensibly, it was what Habib said in an interview with the *Indian Express* on January 13, 1981 that made them intensify their agitation and demand Habib's immediate suspension not only as Dean of the Faculty but also as professor. In the interview, Habib came out with some sordid home truths about his University, saying that 'the criminal elements have intensified the problem by getting into the hostels where they not only get protection but concessions'.[3]

Students began demanding the suspension of Habib for his 'insults'.

> On January 23, the students carried out their protest further to demand an 'assurance' from the vice chancellor that Habib would not be allowed to attend the special convocation for visiting Nobel Laureate Abdus Salam. Two days later the VC is gheraoed and the gherao continues, forcing the VC to close the University *sine die*.[4]

Saiyid Hamid believed that the students' demand for sacking Prof. Habib was unjust, even as he wanted many hostelers who had occupied room for years by virtue of their admission in one course or the other to vacate the rooms. The students, recalls Ishtiaq Ali, didn't understand Saiyid Hamid's intentions. He was a well-wisher of the university and not a corrupt man. He brought the university back from the brink, says Ali. Among the good steps that he took was the revival of the *Tahzib-ul-Akhlaq*, the magazine Sir Syed had brought out soon after his return from England in 1870. The magazine, as we have seen in the earlier chapters, had created a stir in the Muslim society. Saiyid Hamid aptly believed that the magazine was relevant even in these times. 'Saiyid Hamid was a man of modern thinking and scientific approach. He was a product of this university and had imbibed the spirit of the Aligarh Movement. He revived the magazine with a hope to reintroduce the scientific temperament among Urdu readers, especially the AMU community,' recalls retired professor of Urdu Asghar Abbas, who has written extensively on Sir Syed. Abbas had seen Saiyid Hamid very closely and was among his ardent admirers. So, how does he assess Saiyid Hamid's tenure as VC? He says: '*Bus yeh samajh lein ke Syed Hamid ne ek girti huee deewar ko sambhal liya* (Saiyid Hamid saved a crumbling wall). He infused new life into a dying institution.'

Professor Najma Mahmood, who taught English at AMU, was among those who supported Saiyid Hamid to the hilt when many on the campus wanted him to resign. In 1984, she wrote an essay in his support in Urdu, which was later included in her book *Saiyid Hamid: Ke Gum Usmein Hain Afaaq*. Describing Saiyid Hamid's devotion to AMU, she had written:

> Saiyid Hamid is an image of Sir Syed. He has great love for this institution and he can even give his life for it. This is our duty to recognize and respect the greatness of his personality. This is our weakness that we don't see the beauty which is visible to our eyes. Only a jeweller understands the value of a diamond.[5]

As an educationist, Saiyid Hamid was genuinely pained by the educational backwardness of Muslims. He wanted reforms in madrassa education. Since some of the leading madrassas in north India, like the Darul Uloom of Deoband in Uttar Pradesh, didn't seek government support, they also resisted introduction of modern subjects in their curricula. Educationists like Saiyid Hamid favoured the idea that the degrees granted by some of the leading madrassas should be recognized by AMU for allowing them admission. Students from Deoband, Nadwatul Ulema, Lucknow, and a few other madrassas found entry into the 'bastion of modernity'. In the same way that all pass-outs from AMU are called Aligs, the products of these madrassas carry the name of their institution as a badge of honour. So, a product from Deoband is called a Qasmi, as Qasim Nanautvi (1833–1880) was one of the main founders of the Darul Uloom Deoband. A graduate from Nadwatul Ulema in Lucknow is called Nadwi.

Ariful Islam, a retired professor of statistics from AMU, has been noticing the 'infiltration' of madrassa students into AMU for quite some time. 'I too am for reforms in madrassa education. But instead of modernizing the madrassas, they are turning a modern institution like AMU into a madrassa,' he says. He holds Saiyid Hamid responsible for giving an opening to madrassa students, which led to the floodgates being opened for the maulvis to occupy this premier institution of modern education.

If Saiyid Hamid gave a small opening to madrassa students at AMU, Zameer Uddin Shah, vice chancellor from 2012–2017, opened the floodgates to let the maulvis in. Under CPECAMI, he introduced a one-year bridge course for madrassa students. The bridge course has an intake of 100 students, seventy-five boys and twenty-five girls. During the course they are taught English, the humanities, law and information technology. After successful completion of this course, the students are awarded certificates which are equivalent to the certificate of completing the twelfth standard in a standard school. 'The holders of bridge-course certificates can sit for entrance exams for various courses in universities like AMU, JMI and Jamia Hamdard. Many Hafizs (those who remember the Quran by heart) and other Maulvis have joined the mainstream secular courses. Since the madrassas oppose any modernization attempt, this is the only way by which you can modernize some of those who pass out of madrassas. The madrassa students who do this course will enhance their employability in the job market,' says Zameer Uddin Shah, now president of Sir Syed Education Foundation.

The foundation was created while Shah was still VC of AMU, and its purpose was to establish good, English-medium schools as feeder institutions for AMU. 'The serving vice chancellor was supposed to be the foundation's president, but that didn't happen as according to the AMU constitution, it cannot open its schools beyond 25 km from the Jama Masjid at the university. So I remain its president and we have so far established four schools in Uttar Pradesh,' says Shah.

The biggest lacuna bedevilling AMU, says Shah, is the alarmingly poor quality of education at a couple of schools AMU runs. Shah had sacked thirty teachers who were found to be inefficient, but they got reinstated through the courts. 'I found that many teachers at these schools educate their own children at good convent schools but bring them back in the ninth and tenth standards so that they can become internal students and benefit by getting admission in professional courses. Upgradation of these schools is a must to ensure that a pool of good students is provided to the university,' he says.

Shah's term as VC was not without controversies. Among others, one related to denial of permission to girl students to visit the central library of the university, the Maulana Azad Library. It remained in the headlines for many days. At a function at the Women's College, reacting to the demand from girl students for permission to visit the main library, Shah said: 'If you girls are allowed, there will be four times more boys at the library.'[6] In his memoir, *The Sarkari Musalman*,

Shah blames some 'parasites' for recording this statement and feeding it to the media.

Zameer Uddin Shah was called names. Many others faced worse on the campus. Some of the worst cases of violence on the campus are linked to the minority character of the university. The date 25 April 1965 will go down as one of the darkest days in the history of AMU. The Hindu–Muslim ratio of students at AMU had been under debate for quite some time. Contrary to the propaganda some elements keep spreading, there has never been reservation for Muslim students at AMU. However, Badruddin Tayabji, the VC from 1962 to 1965, reserved 75 per cent of the seats for internal students, 'meaning those students who had passed the qualifying examination for a particular class from the university and its allied institutions'.[7] The central government wanted a 50:50 ratio of internal and external students. The government's rationale was that this ratio would impart an all-India character to the university as AMU would attract good students from all corners of the country. But the student community on campus saw the proposal to increase the intake of external students to 50 per cent with suspicion. On 25 April 1965, a meeting of the university's court was being held at the Students' Union Hall when some students barged in and manhandled the members. A rumour had spread that the court had decided to bring down the internal student intake to 50 per cent. Mohammed Adeeb, a former Rajya Sabha member and an alumnus of AMU, who was a student leader and among the group protesting the reduction of the internal intake of students to 50 per cent, recalls the incident:

> Iqbal Hassan Khan, whom I had nicknamed Barula, was the senior proctorial monitor. A day before the meeting

of the university court, Barula had slapped a boy and disappeared. We were looking for him. On the day of the meeting someone said Barula was in the Students' Union Club Hall attending the meeting. Several hundred members had gathered on the ground outside the hall. Many of them barged into the hall looking for Barula. Barula was not there but many court members were manhandled. Three of my friends and I later found the VC Ali Yavar Jung ducking beneath a table. We escorted him out of the hall and were taking him to Sir Syed Hall when a student hit him on the head with a bamboo stick. The VC broke a finger and received many stiches in the head.[8]

However, journalist Anil Maheshwari, in his book *Aligarh Muslim University: Perfect Past and Precarious Present*, gives a slightly different version of the event. He writes:

The Vice Chancellor left the meeting hall for his lodge, but he wrongly turned towards SS Hall. As he had joined the university only a few days ago, he was unfamiliar with its roads and buildings. M.M. Siddiqui, registrar, tried in vain to stop him from turning in that direction. A student swung an iron rod at Jung's head. Instinctively, Jung had placed his hands on his head. The fingers broke as they bore the brunt of the blow. He also sustained as many as 30 wounds on his head. After a few minutes, he resigned under threat to his life. The registrar tried to stop the VC from going towards Sir Syed Hall because hundreds of students were in the hostels and outside their hostels there. The VC lodge is located towards east of the Students' Union Hall. Had the VC walked towards his lodge, he could have escaped the attack from the mob. [9]

Ali Yavar Jung had to resign, virtually at knifepoint, but after his recuperation at a hospital in Delhi he resumed as VC, working mostly from home. Mohammed Adeeb says that seventy-five persons, including the registrar M.M. Siddiqui, were arrested. The registrar was arrested because he had backed the students' demand for seventy-five per cent reservation in admission for internal students as done by Tyabji, Ali Yavar Jung's predecessor. The Centre didn't approve of the incident of violence where a VC was grievously injured. Union Education Minister Mohammadali Carim Chagla decided to whittle down the power of the university court, which until then was the supreme governing body. Through an ordinance the university court was suspended on 20 May 1965. Subsequently, the Aligarh Muslim University (Amendment) Act 1965 was brought in, empowering the 'visitor' (the President of India) to nominate the members of the court, reducing the court to an advisory body. Muslim leaders belonging to different organizations, like the Jamiat Ulama-i-Hind. Jamat-i-Islami (Hind) and the AMU Old Boys' Association, swung into action under the umbrella body of Muslim Majlis-e-Mushawarat. Chagla, a Khoja Muslim from Mumbai, was attacked virulently both by Muslim leaders and the Urdu press. He maintained that AMU was not a minority institution. The Muslim leaders swung into action. They began opposing reduction in the powers of the court.

Another shocker came when, in the Azeez Basha vs Union of India case verdict in 1967, the Supreme Court said that AMU was not a minority institution.

> The Supreme Court rejected the claim of Muslims based upon Article 30(1) of the Constitution mainly on the grounds: (a)AMU was not established by Muslims in as much as it was established by an Act of the legislature and (b)the scheme of the 1920 Act did not confer the exclusive right to administer the university on Muslims.[10]

Years later, this verdict of the Supreme Court became a template for the Allahabad High Court which had challenged the Government of India's permission to AMU to reserve 50 per cent of seats for Muslims in the MS/MD/ post-graduate diploma courses in the faculty of medicine on the plea of thirty-four medical students. On 4 October 2005, the Allahabad High Court quashed the AMU (Amendment) Act, 1981, saying that AMU was not a minority institution. It also said that the 50 per cent reservation for Muslims in post-graduate medical courses was illegal. In 2006, the Aligarh Muslim University challenged the Allahabad High Court's order in the Supreme Court, which stayed the High Court order. The same year, the UPA government filed an affidavit in the Supreme Court supporting AMU's claim for the minority tag. The Modi government, on 6 July 2016, withdrew the UPA-era affidavit. The case still lies in the Supreme Court.

The Supreme Court judgment in the Azeez Basha case created an uproar among Muslim leaders. A leading medical practitioner in Lucknow, Dr Abdul Jalil Faridi, became a champion of AMU's minority-character cause. To mollify the Muslims, Prime Minister Indira Gandhi appointed a cabinet sub-committee, the eight-member Beg Committee, to make recommendations as to the minority character of AMU. The committee articulated the views of the majority of the Muslims when it said:

> Notwithstanding any judgment, decree or order of any court or tribunal to the contrary, Aligarh Muslim University shall be deemed to have been established by the Muslim minority of India as an educational institution of its choice, and shall be administered and managed as provided for in Article 29 and 30 of the Constitution.[11]

Prof. Nurul Hasan replaced M.C. Chagla as education minister and replaced the 1965 act with the Aligarh Muslim University (Amendment) Act, 1972. This act was viewed as more dangerous than the 1965 act, both by the community and the students, as it not only denied the university its minority character, it also reposed too much power in the hands of the vice chancellor. Prof. Nurul Hasan had taught history at AMU before he became a minister. He was liberal and progressive and knew the historic role of the AMU and the sentiments of the Muslims about this university. Yet he recommended what he did. Congress leader Vasant Sathe said that the government did as Nurul Hasan had suggested. Participating in a Parliamentary debate, he said: 'In 1971, the Congress in its manifesto had assured restoration of the minority character to Aligarh Muslim University. We did not do so. We had eminent educationists like Prof. Nurul Hasan who advised us otherwise and we accepted their advice.'[12]

The Aligarh Muslim University (Amendment) Act 1972 received widespread condemnation and strong opposition from the Muslim community. Led by a new body called AMU Action Committee, the movement to establish the university's minority character intensified. Mohammed Adeeb says that this movement birthed a new set of Muslim leaders like Arif Mohammed Khan, Akhtarul Wasey and Javed Habib. All three were students of AMU and plunged into the protests held by the Aligarh Action Committee. 'While we were protesting against Indira Gandhi outside her residence in Delhi, we were arrested and put behind bars at Tihar Jail and were let off after a week,' recalls Akhtarul Wasey, now professor emeritus at Jamia Millia Islamia and president of Maulana Azad University at Jodhpur.[13] Leaders of the Action Committee kept up their protests; then, in May 1973, Akhtarul Wasey and others held a protest in Lucknow. Wasey was detained under the draconian Maintenance of Internal Security Act (MISA), 1971, and had to cool his heels in jail for seven months. If there were some frontline leaders in the community who were against the AMU Amendment Act, 1972, there was also a group that supported Nurul Hasan and opposed the minority character of the university. 'I will not say if Nurul Hasan was eyeing some plum posting and bartered away the university's minority character, but he certainly had a group at Aligarh backing him,' says Wasey. The differences within the teaching staff on the campus on the minority issue were sharp too. 'The so-called "Muslim Group" or the "Rightists" as they were also referred to, led by Professor Rahman Ali Khan of the faculty of law, bitterly opposed the Bill.

On the other hand the "Leftists" and a section of the Congress supporters were backing the Bill.'[14]

When the general elections of 1977 were announced, the Janata Party leaders, including Morarji Desai, who became the prime minister of the first non-Congress government at the Centre, promised Muslims 'that their interests, including the restoration of the original character of AMU, would receive the utmost priority of his government'.[15] The Janata government formed in January 1978 kept dilly-dallying on the minority character of the institution, but constituted the National Minorities Commission. The commission took up the minority character of AMU as its first assignment, rekindling hopes among the AMU community and sympathizers of the university. The commission's chairman was Minoo Masani, and its members M.R.A. Ansari and V.V. John. The commission observed that the AMU (Amendment) 1965 Act severely undermined the university's autonomy. It said:

> If the view taken by the Supreme Court in Azeez Basha's case is correct, it would mean that a religious or linguistic minority is debarred from establishing in as much as a university can only be established by an act of the central or state legislature. We cannot but share the regret of Seervai (a leading constitutional lawyer), which he expressed in these terms—It is the first case in which the Supreme Court has departed from the broad spirit in which it had decided cases on cultural and educational rights of minorities ... It is submitted that the decision is clearly wrong and productive of great public mischief and it should be overruled.[16]

The Janata Party introduced the new AMU (Amendment) Bill in 1979 in the Lok Sabha, but it never went to the Rajya Sabha as the Janata government fell. In the 1979 general elections, every party made restoration of the minority character of AMU part of its poll promise. The Congress government, headed by Indira Gandhi, returned to power in New Delhi. The new Aligarh Muslim University (Third Amendment Bill) was introduced in Parliament on 22 December 1981. A long debate ensued. Participating in the debate in the Rajya Sabha, Syed Shahabuddin, who had resigned from the Indian Foreign Service (IFS) and joined politics, said: 'The Bill, in whatever form it has come, is the culmination of a long struggle, which began 15 years ago when the rights and functions of the university were destroyed by two successive enactments of 1965 and 1972.'[17]

So, after the fifteen-year struggle, the Aligarh Muslim University (Amendment) Act, 1981, was passed. By and large it meets the aspirations of the Indian Muslims, defining the university as the 'educational institution of their choice established by the Muslims of India, which originated as the Muhammadan Anglo-Oriental College, Aligarh and which was subsequently incorporated as the Aligarh Muslim University.'[18] No other Act in the past has bestowed the kind of powers to AMU that this act has. It considers the Muslims of India as a unified body, and the university court, having become the supreme governing body, represents the entire Muslim population of India. Those who were fighting for the all-India status of AMU in the 1920s must have smiled down from above when the AMU (Amendment) Act, 1981, declared, in Section 5(2)C, that it 'empowers the University to promote especially the educational and cultural advancement of the Muslims of India.'[19]

However, Mohammed Sajjad, history professor at AMU, refuses to accept that AMU ever had an all-India status. 'Neither the 1920 Act nor the 1981 Act made AMU an all-India institution. It didn't become a centre of Muslim intellectualism. It looks like a provincial university which, like other universities, hands out degrees,' he says. He adds that the All-India Muslim Educational Conference Sir Syed began in 1866 should have given birth to big institutions in cities like Dhaka, Lahore and Karachi. 'Just as the educational conference became a tool of politics in the hands of Muslim leaders, so has it been the case with AMU,' he says.

The activities that the university began under the act's intent included recognition of madrassa degrees for admission to some courses in the university. This certainly helped the madrassa students, opening up some job options for them, but it also began the 'Madrassanization' of AMU, something its founder Sir Syed Ahmad Khan would not have approved of. It is true that Sir Syed had written to Maulana Qasim Nanautvi, founder of the Darul Uloom Deoband, to send a religious scholar to establish the department of Sunni theology at MAO College. Nanautvi sent a teacher, his own son-in-law Maulana Abdullah Ansari, who became a bridge between Aligarh and Deoband.

The university, in the light of the powers vested in it through the AMU (Amendment) Act, 1981, on 24 February 2005, wrote to the joint secretary in the ministry of human resource development (MHRD), seeking formal approval for reserving 50 per cent of seats for Muslims in the MS/MD and

PG diploma courses in the faculty of medicine. The next day, the joint secretary at MHRD replied: 'This Ministry has no objection to the decision taken by the appropriate authorities of the AMU to reserve 50 % of the total seats in MD/MS/PG Diploma course in the faculty of medicine of the university for Muslims of India on an All-India basis.'[20] But when thirty-four MBBS students petitioned Allahabad High Court in 2005, challenging the government's permission to reserve 50 per cent of seats in the post-graduate medical courses at AMU for Muslims, the Allahabad High Court quashed the AMU (Amendment) Act, 1981, saying that AMU was not a minority institution. The court also called the 50 per cent reservation for Muslims in the post-graduate medical courses illegal. The university challenged the High Court order in the Supreme Court in 2006. The Supreme Court, as mentioned earlier, is yet to give its verdict.

After the United Progressive Alliance (UPA) came to power in 2004, it constituted a high-powered committee headed by a retired judge of the Delhi High Court, Justice Rajinder Sachar, to probe into the conditions of the Muslims in the country. The Sachar Committee made several recommendations to help Muslims out of their backwardness. Then minister of state in the HRD, Ali Ashraf Fatmi, was made head of a thirteen-member committee to examine the various findings of the Sachar Committee in the matter of education and to suggest an action plan. Among other things, the Fatmi Committee said that Aligarh Muslim University should open five campuses across the country. 'These campuses were supposed to be in five states (Kerala, Bihar, West Bengal, Maharashtra and Madhya Pradesh). While centres in Kerala (Malappuram), Bihar (Kishanganj) and West Bengal (Murshidabad) were opened, Maharashtra and Madhya Pradesh didn't allot land for the campuses,' says Ali Ashraf Fatmi, ex-MP from Darbhanga (Bihar) and now a member of the Nitish Kumar-led Janata Dal United (JDU). But what happened to the rule which says that AMU cannot open institutions beyond 25 kms from the university mosque? 'It applies in the matter of schools, not higher institutions. These centres are of higher learning and there the rule doesn't stop AMU from going out and opening its centres,' explains Fatmi, who was a student leader there in the 1980s.

AMU might have opened its off-campus centres, but the main campus has to pull up its socks. It has to retain its reputation as a modern, progressive institution committed to train youths who can uphold rational and scientific thinking. Sir Syed, argues Asghar Abbas, could have easily established a big madrassa if he wanted. He struggled to infuse a new thinking, a rational and scientific temperament, among Muslims. He was opposed by the traditional clerics because he had challenged many set ideas and values. 'I am saddened that they are turning a modern institution into a kind of madrassa with great infrastructure. We will not be doing justice to Sir Syed's legacy and his memories if AMU ends up becoming a madrassa in character even if officially it is a university,' says Abbas.

Some people on the campus are also worried about a new phenomenon, the increasing fault lines due to sectarianism. Though both Shias and Sunnis pray here, and though their prayer times are different, some students and teachers are increasingly avoiding the congregations at the massive Jama Masjid at AMU.

On another occasion, former PRO and the director of Urdu Academy at AMU, Rahat Abrar, was asked to investigate an agitation by a section of the students at the school for the visually-challenged students. Abrar found that a group of boys wanted to go out of the hostel campus and pray at a Sunni mosque in the market because the imam at the mosque in the school premises was a Deobandi. The campus had been clean of such narrow sectarian feelings earlier. Incidents such as these undermine the ideals and values Sir Syed stood for. He had dreamed of founding an institution where Hindus were not forced to observe Muslim religious practices while Muslims were expected to keep their sectarianism aside and put their hearts and minds to grow into a healthy, empowered community.

6

Glorious Past, Precarious Present

IN 2017, late Prof. Shakeel Samdani, who used to teach law at AMU, visited Mumbai to give a talk. Upon finding out that he was in the city, a social group invited him for a chat at P.T. Mane Garden, a civic-run park near Nagpada junction in central Mumbai. They wanted Samdani to speak about the need for an off-campus of the AMU in Maharashtra. AMU, in December 2007, had decided to establish five off-campus centres in the country—in Malappuram (Kerala), Kishanganj (Bihar), Murshidabad (West Bengal), and one each in Maharashtra and Madhya Pradesh. Maharashtra and Madhya Pradesh didn't show interest, even as the rest of the three states allotted land on which building work had begun. Some activists in Mumbai wanted to create awareness among people and put pressure on the state government, and Shakeel Samdani's talk was part of the same awareness campaign.

But even before Samdani stood up to speak, Saeed Khan, a known Muslim activist in Mumbai, began deriding the campaign for an off-campus centre of the AMU in Maharashtra. 'We don't have to do anything with AMU. We don't need (to build) AMU's centre here and antagonize the Maharashtrians, especially Shiv Sena,' Khan said.[1] Samdani was so shocked and put off by this anti-AMU rant that he refused to talk and left.

The activist's ignorance about the historic role AMU has played in the life of Indian Muslims or his deliberate attempt to downsize the varsity and ignore the importance of opening educational centres in areas of substantial Muslim concentration underlines a stark reality. AMU is losing the centrality it enjoyed in the lives of Indian Muslims. It was noted historian Sir Hamilton Alexander Rosskeen Gibb who called Aligarh College 'the first modernist educational institution in the Muslim world.'[2] But over the years, the university has stopped being the 'heartbeat' of Indian Muslims, the 'Qurtaba (Cordoba) of the East', as AMU's first chancellor, Nawab of Bhopal Sultan Jahan Begum, had called the university.

What could be the reasons for Muslims ceasing to see AMU as their 'heartbeat' as earlier generations of Muslims, at least in North India, had? As globalization happened and the economy opened up in the early 1990s, several private and government-funded universities opened in almost every state. Though AMU is one of the central universities, it stopped attracting students from states other than UP and Bihar the way it used to till the 1980s. While talking about AMU losing its grip over the hearts and minds of Indian Muslims, noted poet-lyricist Javed Akhtar once told this writer: 'It is no longer an all-India institution. It looks like a state university of Uttar Pradesh where you have students from Azamgarh, Ballia and

Bahraich.' This may not be entirely true, but AMU undeniably doesn't truly represent the aspirations of Muslims in India today. Since not many students from states other than Bihar and UP get admission here, Muslims in other states don't identify with AMU. They don't show interest in or warmth towards the university and its affairs.

The huge alumni network could be a great strength for AMU if that community were tapped properly. Let us see how approaching and roping in the alumni in recent times brought good dividends to the university. In 2015, Indian-American entrepreneur and philanthropist Frank Islam donated $2 million (around Rs 13 crore) to build the massive Frank and Debbie Islam Management Complex at AMU campus. This is the largest donation made by an individual to AMU. He also donated Rs 1 crore for the state-of-the art auditorium at AMU's department of mass communications. Born in Azamgarh, Frank Islam was fifteen when he left India for the 'American Dream'. He had attended school at AMU before a teacher there helped him leave for America. 'The investment is in the future of America and the American dream and in India as well,' said Frank Islam, who set up the QSS Group, an information technology firm, in 1994 and sold it in 2007 after raising its revenues to over $300 million.[3] Why did Frank Islam donate so much to AMU? 'AMU shaped me in my formative years and helped me become the person I am today. This is my way of repaying the university,' he said.[4]

Another example of an AMU alumnus coming to help his fellow Aligarians was seen during the coronavirus-induced India-wide lockdown announced from 24 March 2020. General secretary of the AMU Alumni Association in Mumbai, Raees Ahmed, announced that any Alig in Mumbai who desperately needed money during the lockdown could approach him privately. Over a dozen approached him, and he helped them with cash, never revealing the names of the beneficiaries to avoid embarrassment to them. This was besides the hundreds of ration kits that he had distributed among the needy. Raees Ahmed was once part of an auction that helped AMU earn several lakhs of rupees. In October 2015, during the World Alumni Meet and Founder's Day, a US-based alumnus, Afshan Hashmi, through video conferencing, put her wedding jewellery on auction at a base price of Rs 6.5 lakh. Raees Ahmed, who was also present at the event, set off the bidding, quoting Rs 11 lakh. He bought the jewellery, and to rousing applause from around 600 alumni from across the globe attending the function, donated it to AMU. 'Wedding jewellery is one of the most cherished possessions of any married woman. It was gifted to AMU with great feeling and emotion, and how could I buy emotions and feelings? What would have I done with jewellery? I donated it to the university,' Ahmed told this author. A Pakistani national too participated in the same auction. 'A donation of $1,000 came from Brigadier (retd) Mohammad Shafi of Pakistan, an AMU alumnus and Pakistan national who too had attended the function.'[5]

In 2014, Raees Ahmed had purchased a set of bangles for Rs 5 lakh in another AMU auction. The bangles were donated to AMU by a Dubai-based woman, an alumnus. After buying them in the auction, Ahmed once again donated the bangles to AMU. Then VC Lt Gen. Zameer Uddin Shah announced that all the jewellery donated to the varsity would be kept at the university museum to encourage and inspire others to do something for their alma mater.

Alumni naturally have a soft corner for their alma mater, though some may be detached towards it too. This writer recently met an alumnus who said he had never returned to the campus since he passed out over a decade ago. And this writer has also met those who celebrate every time AMU makes good news and get edgy and tense if their alma mater is in a crisis. Zohair H. Rizvi was at AMU between 1999 and 2003. He graduated in Urdu and did his master's in business administration (MBA) before he moved to Mumbai, where he is in the perfumery business. He is also the coordinator of the AMU Alumni Association in Mumbai. When the needless controversy over Jinnah's portrait at the Students' Union Hall in AMU had led to violence on 2 May 2018, resulting in six students, including the students' union leader Mashkoor Usmani, getting injured, Zohair Rizvi immediately called up a senior police officer in Aligarh. He knew the officer well and wanted to know why the police had to resort to a lathi charge. The officer told him that had there been no lathi charge, at least half a dozen janaza (corpses) would have gone to Muslim homes that day. Zohair Rizvi recalls the senior officer telling him that some officers were so angry with the students that if the situation had worsened even a little bit more they would have cracked down on the students mercilessly; they were waiting for such an opportunity. The officer also told him that the lathi charge was a deliberate, mild action to force the students to make a retreat and escape fatal injuries should the cops be ordered to fire on them. 'I couldn't sleep that night as I kept thinking about the injuries those six boys had received,' says Rizvi.[6]

A week or so after the lathi charge that day, some members of the AMU Alumni Association, Mumbai, met at General

Secretary Raees Ahmed's office to discuss the situation. Students at AMU were staging an indefinite dharna at the time, while some politicians too were visiting the campus to show solidarity with the students. The students were demanding FIRs to be filed against the goons who had intruded into the campus on 2 May 2018 shouting slogans, and their arrest. The alumni association in Mumbai decided to send a team to Aligarh headed by Fahad Ahmed, AMU alumnus and PhD student at Mumbai-based Tata Institute of Social Sciences (TISS). 'We spoke to a cross-section of people at the campus and especially told the students to end their agitation and concentrate on their studies. I told them that every one of them would become an ambassador for AMU once he or she left the university,' says Fahad Ahmed, who had himself been the general secretary of the students' union at TISS. He also told the AMU students not to see themselves in isolation: 'I told them the alumni community around the world were very concerned about them and they should not do anything that could bring a bad name to the university.'

This feeling of belonging to a larger 'AMU community' used to be cultivated among the students both during the founder Sir Syed's time and for decades afterwards. Till the 1990s, a sort of diversity too was maintained in the allotment of hostel rooms to students. This writer, who was at AMU between 1985 and 1988, remembers being accommodated in a room in Ross Masood Hall which had students from different states and from different streams. This writer shared a room with three others, each from a different state and studying a different subject. So, there was a student from the Unani Medical College, another who was studying engineering, a third graduating in liberal arts while I was in the biology stream in the twelfth standard.

The idea behind housing students from different streams together was to avoid homogeneity and help foster in them an appreciation of diversity. On a visit to the same hostel in 2018, I was shocked to see that all the residents of the hostel were students of engineering, the rationale being that the engineering college was very close to the hostel. This kind of herding doesn't help much to foster a balanced view of life among the young.

Though the Muslim leadership in the country has failed AMU, and especially its student community time and again, the students have routinely sided with the community on many issues. And they have paid for it too. It was proved once again in December 2019. To begin from the beginning, the BJP government at the Centre passed the Citizenship (Amendment) Act, 2019, in the Lok Sabha on 11 December 2019. The Act provides for Indian citizenship for six minorities—Hindus, Buddhists, Sikhs, Jains, Parsis and Christians, but not Muslims—from three countries (Pakistan, Bangladesh and Afghanistan). The act created immense fear, outrage and anger among Muslims and all other peace-loving citizens who believed in the Constitutional guarantee of non-discrimination in citizenship on the basis of religion. 'To compound matters, the act was linked with the NRC by Home Minister Amit Shah, who repeatedly said both in Parliament and in election rallies and television interviews that a Hindu, Buddhist, Sikh, Jain or a Christian left out of the NRC can find his or her name back on it through CAA. He excluded Muslims from the same right, thereby discriminating between citizens of one faith and another.'[7] AMU students had already begun holding discussions on the dangers of the CAA–NRC to Indian democracy. On 10 December, the students took out a candle march to University Circle, the university's end limit. They held a mass hunger strike after the Rajya Sabha passed the CAA on 11 December 2019. Female students participated in large numbers in a protest on 12 December 2019, and on 13 December the students submitted a memorandum to the district magistrate (DM) of Aligarh. Hamza Masood, then a final year LLB student, says that a huge deployment of police and RAF had begun to build at the University Circle, outside the Bab-e-Syed. 'Our protests were completely peaceful. Students protested and even gave their semester and other exams. In all the marches that we took out, the proctorial staff were with us,' recalls Masood, the third generation of his family to have studied at AMU. His uncle Imran Masood is a former MLA. Hamza too aspires to fight the 2022 UP Assembly elections on a Congress ticket.

On 15 December 2019, as news of a heavy lathi charge on the students of Jamia Millia Islamia reached AMU, a group of students gathered at the canteen behind the Maulana Azad Library on the campus. 'A rumour spread that a student had been killed in police firing at JMI. This provoked the students, but they were still peaceful and inside the premises of the University,' says Masood. There were conflicting reports of how the police and rapid action force (RAF) were allowed to enter the campus on the night of 15 December 2019. While the university authorities claimed they feared damage to property at the campus, the students said they were peaceful and that permitting police and RAF to enter the campus was uncalled for. There were reports of tear-gas shelling and lathi charge by the cops.

A fact-finding report prepared by the Karwan-e-Mohabbat and Indian Cultural Forum called the police action 'the Siege of

Aligarh Muslim University'.[8] Led by ex-bureaucrat and writer
Harsh Mander, the fact-finding team comprised members
such as

> 'Nandini Sundar (Professor, Delhi University), John
> Dayal (senior journalist and human rights activist),
> Natasha Badhwar (film-maker), Vimal (human rights
> activist), Ankita Ramgopal (Lawyer, Karwan-e-
> Mohabbat), Sumit Kumar Gupta (Lawyer, Karwan-e-
> Mohabbat), Ishita Mehta (Indian Writers Forum), Varda
> Dixit (Indian Writers Forum), Varna Balakrishnan
> (researcher, Karwan-e-Mohabbat), Syed Mohammad
> Zaheer (Researcher, Karwan-e-Mohabbat), Anwar
> Haque (Karwan-e- Mohabbat) and Sandeep Yadav
> (Photographer, Karwan-e-Mohabbat).'[9]

The fact-finding report was scathing of both the University
authorities and the district administration. 'Their testimonies
(students, teachers of AMU and doctors in the region) revealed
that the university administration, district authorities and the
state government, not only failed in their duty to protect the
campus and its residents against the brutality by the UP police
...' the report read. The report also said that a PhD student lost
his hand after a 'stun grenade' exploded while he was holding it.

> The hand of a PhD student had to be amputated from
> below the wrist due to the injuries sustained from a stun
> grenade that exploded in his hand. By the time this fact-
> finding team reached the campus on 17th afternoon,
> most traces of destruction and explosives had been
> cleaned from the now-desolate university campus,

except for one tear gas shell that we saw still lying in the internal lawns of the Staff Club. In the same video footage shot from the police's end, a policeman is seen holding and then trying to hide a pistol. However, no bullet injuries have been reported. The Registrar also confirmed to us the use of stun grenades, tear gas and water cannons.[10]

The university declared the winter vacation dates after the violence on 15 December 2019. The university would now open only on 5 January 2020. However, the university opened after 13 January 2020 in a phased manner.

Among all the anti-CAA protests at AMU, the one on 12 December 2019 is worth recalling. Among those who spoke on campus that day were Swaraj India founder Yogendra Yadav and Dr Kafeel Khan, the suspended paediatrician of the government-run B.R.D. Medical College and Hospital in Gorakhpur. Dr Khan was a nodal officer at the hospital when over sixty children died in August 2017 from encephalitis-related complications. He was one of the nine people arrested on 2 September 2017 under various sections of the Indian Penal Code (IPC), Indian Medical Council Act and Prevention of Corruption Act for the death of the infants at the hospital. After nearly nine months in jail, Dr Khan was granted bail on 28 April 2018 by the Allahabad High Court, saying that he was not needed in custody since the charge sheet had been filed.[11] On 27 September 2019, 'he was absolved of all charges in the case and an internal hospital enquiry committee cleared him of the allegations.'[12] Meanwhile, on 10 June 2018, an attempt was made on the life of Kafeel Khan's brother Kashif Jameel, who was shot thrice but survived. Dr Khan's is a classic story of a state using its might against its own employee for daring to speak against institutional failures. On 12 December 2019, Kafeel Khan gave a speech at AMU. What did he say in his speech for which the draconian National Security Act (NSA) was invoked against him? Among other things, he said 'Since our childhood we all are taught that we will neither become Hindus nor Muslims, but humans, and our Mota Bhai teaches us that we will become Hindus, Muslims, but not humans.'[13]

The next month, Khan went to meet some anti-CAA activists in Mumbai when the Uttar Pradesh police arrested him at Mumbai airport on 30 January 2020 for his 12 December 2019 speech at AMU, 'saying he made "inflammatory" and "provocative" statements. The FIR was filed under IPC Section 153A.'[14] Though he was granted bail by an Aligarh court on 10 February 2020, Khan was not released and charges under NSA were slapped against him on 14 February 2020. 'The NSA allows the government to detain people for up to one year without a trial if they suspect that they could disrupt public order, endanger the security of India or its ties with foreign countries.'[15]

Restaurateur Farhan Azmi, son of the Samajwadi Party chief and MLA in Maharashtra Abu Asim Azmi, had invited Kafeel Khan to attend an anti-CAA meet held near Radio Club in Colaba, Mumbai, on 28 January. At that rally Farhan Azmi made a controversial remark, saying he too would go to Ayodhya if Maharashtra CM Uddhav Thackeray went there on the completion of 100 days of the Maharashtra Vikas Aghadi (MVA) government. He said:

I demand and I am warning it, consider it as a threat or whatever; if Uddhav Thackeray being the Chief Minister goes to Ayodhya on March 7 (2020) then I will also go along. I will also ask my father to accompany me, I call upon members of MVA and SP members to come along. 'If Uddhav Thackeray confirms his ticket for Ayodhya then we all will hold foot-march to Ayodhya, we will also go along, but the condition is that he will construct Ram Temple and we will construct Babri Masjid.'[16]

After the programme at Colaba, Kafeel Khan went to Bihar to participate in another anti-CAA protest and returned to Mumbai, where he was arrested at the airport on 30 January 2020. 'We had planned to hold a consultation among some of us fellow anti-CAA activists for another protest rally that we were planning. And Kafeel Khan was arrested before he stepped out of the airport,' says Farhan Azmi.

Kafeel Khan spent another seven months in jail before the Allahabad High Court, on 1 September 2020, set aside his detention under NSA and released him from jail. In its verdict the court had said: 'We are having no hesitation in concluding that neither detention of Dr. Kafeel Khan under National Security Act, 1980 nor extension of the detention are sustainable in the eye of law.'[17]

A resident of Gorakhpur, Khan had spent twelve years at Manipal Institute of Medical Sciences at Gangtok.[18] Later he joined BRD Medical College, where he was an assistant professor in the paediatric department.'[19]

The fifteenth of December 2019 became an important day in the history of citizens' resistance against the CAA. This was the day when the Delhi police assaulted students on the Jamia campus. It was also the day when police and RAF personnel entered the AMU campus, allegedly beating up many students and destroying vehicles on the campus. And it was the day that gave birth to the Shaheen Bagh protests. The Shaheen Bagh protests at Road 13A, which links Delhi's Mathura Road with Noida, began on the evening of 15 December 2019 when a group of women sat on a dharna in protest against the police action on Jamia students. The protest, initially by a handful of women at Shaheen Bagh, spawned several Shaheen Baghs in the country.

In contrast, the brutal attack on students at AMU didn't get much coverage in the national media nor find resonance within the Muslim community. Alumni associations in Mumbai, Doha (Qatar) and many other cities did condemn the attack, but both the media and the Muslim community remained riveted to the Shaheen Bagh protests in Delhi and at several Shaheen Baghs elsewhere in the country. Though the fact-finding team led by Harsh Mander had called the police action at AMU 'more brutal than even Jamia',[20] there was not much hue and cry even within the Muslim community against this brutal attack. There was no Dr Syed Mahmud of Patna, Dr Faridi of Lucknow or Syed Shahabuddin hitting the streets as in Delhi and courting arrest to protest against the police excesses at the AMU campus. Since the students were asked to vacate the campus after the winter vacation was announced following the violence on 15 December 2019, there was no way that they could have regrouped to demand justice. And declaration of the coronavirus-induced countrywide lockdown from 24 March 2020 forced all anti-CAA protests, including the one at Shaheen Bagh in Delhi, to shut.

Both the AMU community on campus and its sympathizers outside live mainly in the past glory of the university. They keep talking about how AMU has produced so many heads of states in the subcontinent, for instance. In an article in the monthly magazine *Tahzib-ul-Akhlaq* (March 2021), Jameshed Ahmed Nadwi, an Arabic scholar at Mumbai University, enumerated the various AMU alumni who became heads of states: Indian President Dr Zakir Hussain, Vice President Hamid Ansari, Pakistani President Fazal Elahi Chowdhary, Governor General of Pakistan Sir Khwaja Nazimuddin (he was the second governor general while Mohammad Ali Jinnah was the first), Prime Minister of Bangladesh Mohammed Mansoor Ali and Prime Minister of Pakistan Nawabzada Liaqat Ali Khan. However, he doesn't mention Field Marshal Ayub Khan, the AMU alumnus who became the President of Pakistan. Nadwi also forgets to mention the President of the Maldives, Amin Hilmi Didi, and the ruler of the princely state of Bhopal, Mohd Hameedullah Khan. Other Aligs who adorn the hall of fame include freedom fighters Khan Abdul Ghaffar Khan, Hasrat Mohani, Shaukat Ali and Muhammad Ali, and Raja Mohinder Pratap; Supreme Court Justices Baharul Islam, Syed Murtaza Fazle Ali, S. Sagheer Ahmad and R.P. Sethi; literary heavyweights like Ahmed Ali, Raja Rao, Ale Ahmad Suroor, Saadat Hasan Manto, Ali Sardar Jafri, K.A. Abbas, Shaharyar, Asrarul Haque Majaz; actors Naseeruddin Shah and Saeed Jaffrey; lyricists Shakeel Badayuni and Javed Akhtar; playback singer Talat Mehmood; test cricketers C.S. Naidu and Syed Mushtaq Ali; and Olympians Aslam Sher Khan, Govinda and Zafar Iqbal.[21] These are but few names from a long list of men and women who have brought laurels to the university. But most of them are from the pages of history.

The current situation is not such a happy one as far as AMU's ranking among Indian universities is concerned. Under the National Institutional Ranking Framework (NIRF), AMU slipped from the eighteenth rank in 2019 to thirty-first in 2020 in overall ranking in India, while among Indian universities it slipped to the seventeenth rank in 2020 from eleventh in 2019. However, AMU was ranked fourth among government universities (general) in India in the rankings for 2021 by *India Today* magazine.

One of the parameters by which to fathom the excellence of a government-funded university like AMU is the performance of its students in the civil services exams that the Union Public Service Commission (UPSC) conducts for selection of IAS, Indian Foreign Service, Indian Police Service and allied services. AMU already had a coaching and guidance centre before it was merged with the residential coaching academy (RCA) established in 2010 as per the University Grants Commission (UGC) scheme for establishment of such academies for minorities, scheduled castes and communities, and women. Despite AMU's great infrastructure, including its own rich library and the university's Maulana Azad Library, the performance of the RCA at Aligarh has been less than satisfactory. Syed Zafar Mahmood, AMU alumnus, former civil servant, former member of the executive council at AMU and founder-president of the Zakat Foundation of India, once raised a question at an executive committee meeting about the poor performance of RCA Aligarh. He was asked to diagnose the disease and give suggestions for its improvement. 'I suggested several steps ... I told them that the catchment area for the intake students (100) for residential coaching and guidance should be expanded. Even if a candidate who is not a student of AMU but qualifies in their entrance test for the RCA, he/she should be selected for coaching. Secondly, the director of the academy should not be any working or retired professor. He should be someone who has qualified in one or two levels of the UPSC exams even if he was not selected finally. The third suggestion was that the faculty to teach at RCA should not be the university teachers but professionals who teach at different coaching institutes in Delhi,' says Zafar Mahmood, who was also part of the Sachar Committee, which inquired into the social, economic and educational condition of Muslims in India. Its report was submitted in 2006.

Mahmood says that he has been writing to the VCs at AMU since 2006 about improving the performance of AMU students at competitive examinations. His pleas have fetched little attention. Mahmood recalls how, after he had cracked the civil services exams in 1977, he would often visit AMU on Sundays and address students at the hostel dining halls. Once, a student, Rizwan Ahmed, was prodded by a friend into attending one of the talks. He was reluctant and wanted to sleep that Sunday afternoon. But somehow, Rizwan Ahmed found himself sitting through Zafar Mahmood's lecture. He found it so inspiring that he began preparing for the exams, cracked them and joined the IPS. He was placed in the Uttar Pradesh cadre, from where he retired as director general of police (DGP) in 2014.

Zafar Mahmood too has been a victim of the communal virus and Islamophobia infecting Indian society. For the last decade or so, his NGO Zakat Foundation of India (ZFI) has arranged for coaching and guidance for some Muslim candidates for the civil services exams. In August 2020, a private news channel, Sudarshan TV, created a multi-episode show 'Bindas Bol—UPSC Jihad,' 'the promo of which had claimed that the channel would air a "big exposé on the conspiracy to infiltrate Muslims in government services".[22]

On 15 September 2020, the Supreme Court restrained the channel from further telecasting the show (it had already telecast two episodes). The top court observed that 'the intent' of the episodes 'prima facie' appeared to 'vilify' the Muslim community. In one of the episodes created by Sudarshan TV's anchor and editor-in-chief Suresh Chavhanke, it was alleged that Zakat Foundation of India, which helps Muslim candidates crack the civil services exams, 'was receiving funding from foreign "anti-India organisations"'.[23] Speaking to The Wire, Mahmood had said 'the narrow thought process displayed by Sudarshan TV was an "aberration" and that "over 95% of the population would never subscribe to such radical views".'[24]

'He also denied all the allegations of financial wrongdoing, and said that his foundation has regularly fulfilled all the fairness rules prescribed by the ministry of home affairs, in addition to adhering to the Foreign Contributions Regulation Act and income tax laws.'[25]

'It was an attempt to discourage us from continuing good work which is lawful, legitimate and towards empowering the minorities. If anything, it has only emboldened us to go ahead with our modest programme,' says Mahmood.

The credit goes to an Alig like Zafar Mahmood for taking the lead in helping Muslim students crack the civil services exams. Now he has diversified the services Zakat Foundation provides. Apart from providing help to UPSC aspirants, the Foundation has also begun helping aspirants prepare for the State Civil Services Exams and the competitive tests for Staff Selection to government services too.

The decline in AMU began in the last decade of the twentieth century, especially during the tenure of M.N. Farooqui (1990–1994). Asghar Abbas says that Saiyid Hamid and his immediate successor Syed M.N. Faruqi restored order and created an atmosphere for intellectual development at AMU. The situation was not too bad even during the tenure of VC M. Rahman (1995–2000)—an ex-IAS officer of the Jammu and Kashmir cadre who succeeded Hashim Ali—though Rahman was accused of surrendering to the saffron ideology when he joined the Atal Bihari Vajpayee Himayat Committee, an organization created in 2004 to shore up support for the Vajpayee-led BJP. Rahman had told this writer an interesting story after he had completed his term as VC. He said that Kalyan Singh, in his second term (1997–99) as chief minister of UP, was visiting Aligarh and he wanted to visit the university campus too. Rahman, despite opposition from a section of staff and students, hosted the CM for a few hours. The then district magistrate of Aligarh was also present at this meeting. Rahman told Kalyan Singh that since the main road that went through the campus, joining it from south to north, belonged to the UP government, regular traffic could also pass through it, and that this was leading to accidents and allowing anti-social elements access to the campus. Kalyan Singh heard the plea patiently and ordered the collector to transfer ownership of the road to the university soon. Since there were many other roads providing the same connectivity in the region, the collector had no problem in signing the documents and handing over the road's ownership to Rahman in a couple of months. Rahman got a beautiful gate built at the southern entry point of the university, the Bab-e-Syed. However, former PRO Rahat Abrar says he doesn't remember Kalyan Singh ever visiting AMU campus. He adds that there was a government guest house near the campus and VC M. Rahman might have met Kalyan Singh there.

Deputy Director of Sir Syed Academy at AMU, Dr Mohammed Shahid gives a slightly different version. He says that Kalyan Singh visited Aligarh to unveil the portrait of Dr B.R. Ambedkar at the Ambedkar Park near the district magistrate's office, close to the AMU campus. Dr Rahman was also present at the programme. 'He might have raised the issue as there was a general talk on the campus that day and local newspapers reported next day that the university road had been officially handed over to the university,' he says.

However, the early 1990s had seen a decline in law and order at the university, affecting its academic atmosphere. 'Nepotism in recruitment, especially in the appointment of teaching staff, was a major contributory factor leading to the decline in academic standards ... The law-and-order situation at AMU had reached its nadir in the early nineties. Between 1991 and 1996, armed gunmen shot two senior teachers dead inside the university campus and the cases were never fully solved. In both cases the hand of land mafia was suspected.'[26]

Dr Hamid Ansari, AMU alumnus, former diplomat and vice president, took over as AMU vice chancellor in 2000. In an address to the AMU court, Ansari had tried to diagnose the disease that ails AMU. He said:

The University is a living organization and cannot subsist only on nostalgia and past glory. The AMU and AMU community of students, teachers, alumni and well-wishers have to face squarely the challenges of modern India and of the 21st century. Foremost among these is the emphasis on quality; a high degree of competition is thus inevitable. The problem of numbers is an impediment. A residential University meant for about six thousand students of whom seventy-five per cent were required to reside in the halls of residence has grown in size beyond recognition and without adequate planning.[27]

The university deserves a strong, visionary leadership which can withstand political pressure and safeguard the students' interests. A VC is like the head of a family and the students his/her children. He/She should have the courage to reach out to the students and talk to them if they have any grievances. Calling the cops at the drop of a hat and treating agitating students as 'enemies' is not a healthy sign. AMU, like any liberal university, should give the student community the right to dissent. If its past was glorious, its present should not be precarious.

7

The Tablighi Footprint

THE knock on the door was gentle. As I opened it, I saw four or five kurta-pyjama-clad bearded men in skull caps standing before me. '*Asalamu alaikum*,' said the leader of the group, holding out his right hand to shake. This was the first time I had ever seen members of the Tablighi Jamaat, or preachers' party.

I was an eleventh-standard student and had recently joined Aligarh Muslim University (AMU) in 1985. The leader of the group standing outside my hostel spoke softly and sermonized briefly. He said that life on this earth was transitory. The real life lay in the hereafter and we had to prepare for that life. The preparation had to be done while we lived here. And then he invited me to my hostel mosque. More out of curiosity than devotion, I accompanied the group.

We knocked at a few more rooms, the leader of the group mechanically repeating the rehearsed lines about life's transitory character and the permanent address we all are destined to get in the hereafter. Since we were meeting students, many examples set in student life featured in the talks. So, this life is like an examination hall. Our performance here will decide our grade of life in the hereafter. As the time for maghrib, or evening namaz, approached, we moved to the hostel's mosque. After the farz, or mandatory three-unit evening prayer, a middle-aged man with a flowing beard stood up and asked the worshippers to stay back for a while after finishing their remaining prayers. Some heeded his call while others finished their remaining prayers and exited. Those who stayed back were requested to move forward and sit close to each other.

The middle-aged man who began speaking to this group of listeners was the ameer, the head of the jamaat or party of Tablighis who had come from outside the town. Speaking softly, the ameer stressed the need for making sacrifices in Allah ki raah (God's way). And the sacrifices included those of money and time. No, the Jamaat doesn't collect any chanda or donation. They never say they want money because a mosque has to be built or some poor need to be fed. They never express concern for illiteracy, poverty, unemployment, drug abuse and so many other ills that bedevil the community.

The students were told that they needed to take time off from their schedule—since here their targets were university students, the students needed to halt their studies for a couple of days—and join a jamaat for a short trip of three days outside the town. They were told that they would self-fund their trip, carry their own kerosene-powered stoves (gas cylinders were not popular then), cook their own food and avoid making any demands of food or money on the locals they interacted with during their short trip. During their stay outside their homes/hostels for three nights, they would spend their time in zikr (remembering the creator) and fikr (worrying about life in the hereafter). The newcomer, like this writer, was taught a few verses of the Quran which are recited in namaz. We were also told about the different rituals of namaz: how to stand for prayers, what to recite at different stages of namaz, how to bow down. After three days of living outside the hostel at a mosque in a small village near Aligarh town, we returned. I was told to attend the jamaat meetings regularly. But to the dismay of my fellow travellers on that short trip of three days, I never joined their party again.

That was my first and last trip with the Tablighis. The missionary zeal with which they entice newcomers is tribute to their patience. Without holding out the lure of money or promising people comfortable stays—the participants have to sleep on hard, coarse bedding, like a duree, laid out on the floor of a mosque—they manage to attract youths as well as grown-up men. In big metros, small towns and villages, a familiar sight in Muslim mohallas is a group of bearded men, mostly in loose kurta-pyjamas, carrying bags on their backs and exiting or entering a mosque. Mostly they are Indians, but occasionally they are foreigners too. These bearded men are on a mission—a mission to correct themselves, prepare and purify themselves before they exit this world and journey to another world. Time is short. Life is transitory, it is ephemeral. All the comforts and joys on this earth are too transient to become life's ultimate goal. No king or emperor has ever lasted forever. The pharaohs in ancient Egypt once possessed enormous power. Today their remains are visible only in some mummies in museums. Such examples often featured while I stayed with the group for three days. I was young, my sensibilities were raw. Out of curiosity, tinged with a bit of adventure and search for divine blessings, I swam with the flow, even if the swimming was very brief.

Little did I know that these publicity-shy, inward-looking, luxuriantly bearded men in long kurtas and short pyjamas would one day hit the headlines for the wrong reasons. Little did I know that the national media would debate so incessantly, so aggressively, this group of Muslims for so many days. These Muslims are so escapist that they talk about life beneath the earth and beyond the sky. And yet the Tablighis at the end of March and early April 2020 found themselves at the centre of a controversy.

The Tablighi Markaz, the erstwhile Banglewali Masjid in Nizamuddin, Delhi, is just a few feet away from the shrine of the famous Sufi saint Hazrat Nizamuddin Auliya (1238–1325). A famous mystic of his time, Nizamuddin Auliya stressed love for mankind and aloofness from worldly pleasures. I am not sure if even a fraction of the thousands who throng the markaz and its masjid are interested in visiting Nizamuddin Auliya's shrine just a stone's throw away. Not much is common between the hordes who seek solace at the Sufi saint's fourteenth-century shrine and the thousands who visit the Nizamuddin Markaz of the Tablighis every day to receive guidance on how to become a good Muslim on earth. Puritanical Islam discourages visits to the tombs and shrines of Sufi saints. Since the Tablighis are ideologically close to the Deobandis, who oppose pilgrimage to the shrines of Sufi saints, they too don't follow the Sufi practice of sama or Sufi qawwali at the shrine of Nizamuddin Auliya or at any other Sufi shrine. Unlike other Sunni Muslims, like the Barelvis, the Tablighis don't believe in the intercession of any human in seeking divine help. The Barelvis revere saints and visit the tombs of Sufi saints in the subcontinent. The difference between the Tablighi and the Barelvi is deep. This difference prevails on the AMU campus too. Followers of the Barelvi sect don't offer namaz under the leadership of Deobandi or Tablighi imams. At many places in Maharashtra and Uttar Pradesh, many Barelvi mosques carry notices outside banning entry to Deobandis, Tablighis and Wahabis. Many Barelvis discourage the participation of Tablighis and Deobandis in their wedding ceremonies and in the namaz-e-janaza, or funeral, of their members.

Dwarfed under the shadow of the massive building of the markaz is the tomb of the famous Urdu-Persian poet Mirza Asadullah Khan Ghalib (1797–1869). As the cops and agencies swooped down on the Tablighi Markaz to evacuate over 2,000 members of the Tablighi Jamaat from the markaz, the poet Ghalib must have mumbled some of his own timeless lines that describe the everyday drama of life as it unfolded before his eyes: *'Bazeecha-e-atfal hai duniya mere aage/ Hota hai shab-o-roz tamasha mere aage'* (The world to me is like a child's playground/The play of life is enacted endlessly before me)'

Ghalib, who never had pretensions about his devoutness, must have found comfort in his own iconoclasm, his irreligiosity, as the religious men at the markaz were picked up and sent to various quarantine centres in the city. We will come to that episode a little later in this chapter.

Like so many other Indian Muslim movements, the Tablighi Jamaat movement too received traction at AMU, the supposed centre of progressive and liberal Muslims. Since they get a huge chunk of young Muslims at one place, the Tablighis could not have remained behind in popularizing their movement among the AMU community. Where else on earth could they have found so many educated Muslims all assembled in one small township? AMU had the raw power of youth and many mosques, including the massive Jama Masjid that sits on the quadrangle of MAO College which founder Sir Syed Ahmad Khan had created. There has always been a tussle between the orthodox and the progressives on the campus. The men and women of God have fought the godless groups. As the grip of communists and their ideological fellow travellers on sections of the student community weakened, the Tablighis filled the space. We will discuss how Aligarh helped form or popularize other Islamic movements—like the Jamaat-e-Islami Hind (JIH), Jamiat Ulama-i-Hind, Students' Islamic Movement of India (now banned), Students' Islamic Organization (SIO), Muslim Majlis-e-Mushawarat and the All-India Muslim Personal Law Board—in the next chapter. Here we confine ourselves to exploring the Tablighis' influence on the AMU community and the extent to which the university helped the movement to grow.

The freshers are the first targets of the Tablighis. The Tablighis approach the freshers with the lure of learning about the faith away from their hostels, away from their classrooms and their textbooks. The fact remains that in the Jamaat they teach newcomers little beyond a few suras or Quranic verses that are recited in namaz. Of course, the newcomers are given sermons and a heavy, boring dose on why this world is transitory and like a station in one's life's journey while man's final destination is in the hereafter. They neither talk about the spiritual and philosophical aspects of religion nor discuss the features of political Islam. The focus is on attaining purity, a certain discipline, mainly through performing namaz regularly. Out of the five pillars of Islam— shahda, or declaration that God is one and Muhammad is His prophet; namaz; roza, or fasting during the month of Ramzan; Haj (annual pilgrimage to Mecca obligatory only for those who can afford it), and zakat (donating 2.5 per cent of one's savings to charity)—the Jamaatis or Tablighis focus more on namaz than on any other duty that Islam desires of its adherents. I realized only much later why they insisted on the learning of the suras or the holy verses that are required to be recited during the performance of namaz. I didn't realize it immediately after I had left my hostel room to accompany the team of Jamaatis—for the first and last time—years ago.

Since namaz is considered the most important farz or mandatory duty for a Muslim, the maximum efforts of the Jamaatis go into imparting the message that come whatever difficulty, namaz should not be abandoned. The new recruits are told time and again that they should make namaz a feature of their twenty-four-hour routine and that offering namaz five times a day should get priority over everything else. Some Jamaatis become so habituated to this routine that they roll out their prayer mats at railway stations, airports and even on their train berths when they are on long journeys. Namaz is seen as and made so central to life that they can go hungry and thirsty but will not forego it. This strict adherence to namaz comes from practice, we are told. Taking time off to visit different places in groups called jamaats is basically to enable practice of the different sessions of namaz with utmost concentration, away from home and hearth, factory and farm, college and classroom. This practice makes the members 'namazis'—those who offer namaz regularly. Once they get addicted to it, they will seldom give it up. Namaz stays with devout Muslims till the end.

Raisuddin Ansari had joined the bachelor of engineering (BE) course, at that time a five-year programme, at AMU in 1978. He says that his father was associated with the Tablighi Jamaat in his native Gorakhpur, so the Jamaat was not new to him. Why did he get so attracted to it? '*Yeh Jamaat apne aap ko jawab deh banata hai* (This Jamaat makes one accountable to oneself). It tells you that you have to take responsibility for everything,' he says. He explains that the Tablighi Jamaat basically does two things. It instils fear of Judgement Day and creates an urge for Jannah, or paradise. Since Islam believes in Judgement Day and clearly says that good deeds will be rewarded with heaven and bad deeds punished with hellfire, the Tablighis play on the fear of that severe punishment that awaits those who will dwell in hell. And if eternal hellfire is to be avoided, people must fulfil the duty that God has prescribed for them. And to learn about those duties that the Jamaat insists on, trips away from home for three days, twelve days or forty days are advisable.

Shahid Tandon was a student at AMU in the late 1980s. He remembers that whenever he or some of his other friends saw the Jamaat members coming towards their hostel, they would try to hide. Some would bolt their rooms from inside and feign sleep when they heard the knocks on their doors. Many hid inside toilets till the 'Allah ki fauj' (army of Allah) gave up looking for their 'shikar' (prey). Army of Allah? Yes, Tablighis are called that by many students at Aligarh. Tandon is among those who bemoan the colossal loss of the community's human resources as a result of the engagement of so many educated individuals in this Tablighi work. 'To me it seems a sheer waste of time and energy. One can understand that the unlettered join the Jamaat to learn a few rituals and verses that are used in namaz. Why should students and scholars waste their time in an activity that never talks of educational or economic empowerment of the community?' says Tandon.[1]

Empowering the subcontinent's Muslims with modern education and scientific thinking was at the core of Sir Syed's movement. Yet the beneficiaries of Sir Syed's benevolence, the Tablighis, never talk about these things in their meetings. They don't discuss the economic, educational and social backwardness of the community. The book important to the Tablighis is *Fazail-e-Amal* by Maulana Zakariya (1898–1982). The book mainly talks about the five pillars of Islam. The hadiths or traditions of the Prophet in this book are narrated with anecdotes. The primacy of *Fazail-e-Amal* can be gauged from the fact that 'no meeting ever draws to a close without either reading or at least a mention of Fazail-e-Amal, which is read at least twice a day in any mosque under the influence of the Tablighi Jamaat.'[2]

Aligarh has the biggest concentration of educated Muslims in the world. A chunk of them are members of the Tablighi Jamaat, even though the organization does not offer formal membership. No register keeps details of the people who have joined the movement over the decades; or of those who came, spent some time with the mission, but got disenchanted and left. The monotony with which the Jamaat conducts its functions can baffle any individual of sound education and intelligence. Yet, the number of precious hours these educated members of the community spend on travelling to near and far-off places for Tablighi work is huge. Had this educated class, which spends so much time and money on travelling, concentrated on studying science and the arts, in research and experimentation, they could have brought about a revolution. One doesn't suggest that they give up learning the rituals, offering prayers, reciting the Quranic verses or propagating the faith. But adopting an escapist, isolationist attitude towards life is harmful for the community's growth.

Shahid Tandon remembers how a senior professor on the campus spent a lot of time on Tablighi work, ignoring his own family. 'Whenever he got a chance, he would go out of town on Tablighi work. He was so addicted to it that a joke spread that he was a part-time professor,' says Tandon.

However, Mumbai-based Zafar Sareshwala, businessman and a former chancellor of Maulana Azad National Urdu University (MANUU), Hyderabad, disagrees that Tablighis teach escapism, or that they waste the faithfuls' time and energy. Sareshwala's father was an IITian and had spent decades in the Tabligh. Sareshwala also refuses to accept that it is mainly the poor and illiterate who join the Tablighi movement. Sareshwala says he did a whole chilla, or forty-day trip, in the Tabligh at the AMU campus in 1989. Moving from mosque to mosque in the different halls of residence, he met students and teachers and observed residential life on the campus from close quarters. He says he once heard a story about how the Tablighis found their foothold in Aligarh. Maulana Mian Mehrab, among the earliest followers of the Tablighi Movement founder Maulana Ilyas, had told Sareshwala this story.

In the 1940s, Sareshwala said, a Tablighi Jamaati visited AMU. Perhaps it was one of the earliest Jamaatis to visit the campus. Those days, most of the AMU students wore sherwani and churidar; many came from aristocratic families and would not suffer the uneducated easily. When the students found a group of simpletons as part of Tablighi Jamaat in their midst, they wanted to play pranks on them. The students got the group into a room and closed the door from outside after switching on the ceiling fan. It was December. The villagers didn't know how to switch off the fans as they had never seen one before. They spent the freezing night praying to God that the Tabligh should take strong root in the university. The story sounds apocryphal, but the Tabligh movement did take deep root on the AMU campus. Its footprints are visible everywhere on the campus.

Prof. Abdul Aleem of the statistics department, Prof. Khalid from the Persian department in the 1970s, Prof. Sanaullah, again from the statistics department, Prof. Salman Beg from the engineering department in the 1980s and many other senior teachers became big promoters of the Tabligh movement on and off the campus. 'As students and teachers of AMU moved out of the campus and went to different parts of the world, they took the Tabligh too with them. I have met AMU students and teachers doing Tabligh work in Australia, Germany, England, the US and Malaysia. AMU gave big support to the Tabligh movement as more educated Muslims joined it, and the same volunteers spread the movement,' says Sareshwala. He cites the example of Malaysia, which sent hundreds of students to study at universities in England and America, to find that many of them returned as professionals (doctors, engineers, lawyers, management graduates) who were also indoctrinated in Tabligh philosophy. 'Malaysian PM Dr Mahathir Mohamad wondered how these students, whom the government sent to study, became ardent followers of the Tabligh, and they too set up a strong network of the Tabligh in Malaysia,' says Sareshwala. He agrees that the Tablighis never discuss politics or controversial issues at their sessions in mosques or on the streets. 'They are more concerned about cleaning hearts than cleaning the Augean stables that politics has created,' explains Sareshwala.

True, the Tablighis never discuss politics, issues like denial of justice to the innocent or the backwardness of the community, by almost any parameter. When the police used brutal force to suppress the anti-CAA protests at Jamia Millia Islamia, in UP and elsewhere in the country, when the grannies of Shaheen Baug were occupying a part of a road in Delhi and the world media had turned their focus on their unique movement, and when the police entered the AMU campus on the night of 15 December 2019, beating many of the students who had assembled to protest the assault on students reading at Jamia Millia Islamia's library earlier in the evening, the Tablighis kept quiet. All other Muslim organizations condemned the incidents. The Tablighis didn't find it fit to even issue a press release, didn't hold a press conference and didn't join the activists to chant slogans at Delhi's Jantar Mantar. They were and are not concerned about the existential issues of the community or the country. They are more worried about the life hereafter and work towards that end.

How and where did the Tablighi Jamaat begin its journey? Maulana Muhammad Ilyas Kandhalwi (1884–1944) was a student at Darul Uloom Deoband in UP when he heard about some Muslims getting converted to Hinduism as they were weak in their faith. He began teaching at the Madrassa Mazahirul Uloom in Saharanpur, also in UP. In the 1890s, Swami Dayanand Saraswati began his Shuddhi campaign in which neo-Muslims were reconverted to Hinduism. In many villages of Haryana, Punjab, Rajasthan and Uttar Pradesh, some poor, illiterate neo-

Muslims, who had retained their earlier customs and culture even though they had embraced Islam, were coming under the influence of the Shuddhi campaign. Saraswati's campaign focused on these neo-Muslims and began reconverting many of them to Hinduism. Though Tablighis don't proselytize, they may have stopped many neo-Muslims from returning to their old faith. Maulana Ilyas's movement succeeded, because he initially worked with these poor, illiterate Muslims who were likely to be persuaded to reconvert. The Tablighis began telling the poor that poverty was not a bane. They didn't celebrate poverty but didn't speak against it either. What is more tragic is dying without knowing the faith Prophet Muhammad had brought them, the Tablighis told the illiterate and the poor, and continue to tell them to this day. The rich were asked to sacrifice their time and the poor were persuaded to spend a part of their hard-earned money in Khuda ki raah (Way of God).

Unlike other organizations where hierarchy counts, in the Tablighi Jamaat there are no formal posts to be grabbed. It is true that there has been a running feud over control of the Jamaat between Maulana Saad and the Shura, or the advisory council. The Shura members broke away from the main group in 2017, accusing Maulana Saad of usurping the post of Ameer, or head, and found their bases at a mosque in Old Delhi and at another mosque in Nerul near Mumbai. The followers of Maulana Saad outnumber the followers of the six-member Shura, which consists of two members from Pakistan, one from Bangladesh and three from India.

Still, when it comes to enjoying facilities on trips in India or abroad, everyone in the group is equal. Even the Ameer, or the head of the Jamaat, eats the same food that the other volunteers in the team do. No special treatment is accorded to the Ameer.

Since the Tablighis are ideologically close to the Deobandis, they get favourable reception among the huge mass of Deobandi Muslims across the country and the world. The Deobandi mosques are open to the Tablighis as they almost always stay at mosques and not at private accommodations. They pay for their own food and travel. Very rarely do they accept invitations to lunch or dinner that may be offered during their trips.

Maulana Ilyas visited Mecca for the second time in 1924, and the inspiration to start Tabligh work came during this visit. Ziya Us Salam, in his book *Inside the Tablighi Jamaat,* writes:

> In 1924, Ilyas had gone to Mecca and stayed there for five months. As he weighed the pros and cons of settling there, he received a vision from Prophet Muhammad who commanded him to go back to India where Allah would give him work to do. Illyas returned to India soon after, confident he was destined to work for his faith. In his mid-twenties, Ilyas is believed to have had another vision in a dream—this time regarding the methodology of preaching. He is said to have based the division of proselytization work within the community on this vision.[3]

Ilyas gave up his teaching job at Madrassa Mazahirul Uloom in Saharanpur and relocated to Nizamuddin in Delhi, where his father Maulana Mohammad Ismail ran a madrassa, Madrassa Kashiful Uloom. Legend has it that Maulana Ismail would pay some money to the poor Meos or Muslims of the Mewat region in Haryana who visited Delhi in search of work, just for spending time at the mosque and learning the rituals of namaz. Word of this spread, and soon more poor villagers from

Haryana flocked to the mosque. This way the Meos became the initial grass-roots workers when Maulana Ilyas took over the madrassa after the death of his father and his brother Muhammad. The Meos or Muslims of the Mewat region in Haryana approached Maulana Ilyas with a request to run the madrassa his father had established. His father had left behind a circle of disciples among the Meos. Ilyas also began setting up elementary schools for the Meos who were already in touch with him as a result of that madrassa.

In 1927, Ilyas began the Tablighi Jamaat movement from Nizamuddin. The idea was to return to the puritanical ways of the time of the Prophet. Since he was upset to see Muslims carrying huge cultural influences from their former faiths, he created a slogan '*Musalmanon, Musalman bano* (Muslims, be Muslims).'[4] Since a large number of Meos in Haryana were former Rajputs and many were returning to their former faith because they didn't find the new one very attractive, and also because of the Shuddhi campaigns, Ilyas began sending small Jamaats or teams of four and five people to call them to prayer at the local mosques. 'Over the next hundred years or so, around 150 countries of the world embraced the organization which, ironically, shuns the world!'[5]

Ninety-three years after it was founded in Nizamuddin, the Tablighi Jamaat and its markaz, or headquarters, found themselves caught in a storm. The Islamic movement, which had shunned publicity and never had a PR or media wing, was debated in the media ad nauseum for days. The Tablighis and the markaz at Nizamuddin had hit the headlines for the wrong reasons. 'The Tabligh was pronounced guilty of hosting an international meeting of preachers from 13 to 15 March which was attended by more than 3,000 men.'[6]

On 30 March 2020, the news 'broke' that the Tablighi Markaz had begun a 'Corona jihad', (Corona terrorism), against the Indian state, as it had 'hidden' 3,000 Tablighis on its premises. Nobody bothered to understand that Prime Minister Narendra Modi had announced a complete lockdown with effect from the midnight of 24/25 March and that the Tablighis too were stranded, like many others across the country. It is not that they had not tried to vacate the premises before they were 'caught huddled' at the markaz. Before the senior leaders of the Jamaat could even explain their innocence, they were pronounced guilty. The Islamophobic media presented the whole development as though the Muslims had deliberately started a 'Corona jihad' against the country. On 31 March 2020, the markaz issued a clarification:

When the Prime Minister announced the Janata Curfew for March 22, the ongoing programme in the Markaz was discontinued immediately. However, due to the sudden cancellation of railway services across the country on March 21, a large number of visitors got stuck in the Markaz premises. Before the Janta curfew could be lifted, the Chief Minister of Delhi announced a lockdown of Delhi, beginning at 6 am on March 23. On the evening of March 24, a further nationwide lockdown was announced by the Prime Minister with a clear message for people to stay put wherever they were. Under such compelling circumstances there was no option for the Markaz but to accommodate the stranded visitors with prescribed medical precautions until the situation became conducive for their movement or arrangements were made by the authorities.[7]

On the morning of 1 April 2020, the Tablighis were evacuated and bused to different quarantine centres in Delhi. They were accused of many misdemeanours, like sneezing, spitting, urinating and defecating in the open so as to spread infections. The Tablighi Jamaat's chief, Maulana Saad, 'disappeared' for three weeks. This only added fuel to the anti-Tablighi propaganda. Many news outlets focused on his farmhouse at Kandhla in Shamli district, Uttar Pradesh, and gave the impression that the head of the Jamaat had amassed huge wealth.

The bias of the Indian government towards the Tablighis who had attended the mid-March meeting at the markaz was also evident in the way the Ministry of Home Affairs directed the police to file cases against them.

On 1 April, the MHA blacklisted 960 foreigners and cancelled their visas, alleging that their involvement in the Tablighi Jamaat event violated their visa conditions. The home minister's office had asked the Delhi Police and police chiefs of other states, where these foreigners were currently living, to take legal action under the Foreigners Act and the Disaster Management Act.[8]

The Tablighis were slapped with cases.

On completion of the investigation, 48 chargesheets and 11 supplementary chargesheets were filed arraying 953 foreign nationals of 36 different countries as accused. They were charged with violating visa rules, government guidelines issued in the wake of the pandemic, Epidemic Diseases Act and Disaster Management Act rules and prohibitory orders under Section 144 of the Code of Criminal Procedure. They were also booked for the offences under Sections 188, 269, 270 and 271 (disobedience to quarantine rule) of the IPC and relevant sections of the Foreigners Act.[9]

Despite their humiliation and harassment, many Tablighi volunteers who had tested positive for COVID-19 and recovered after treatment voluntarily donated life-saving plasma. They didn't dwell on the fact that just a month or so ago they were called 'super spreaders' of the virus and were accused of waging a 'Corona jihad' against India.

They were subsequently let off, with the judges reprimanding the officials for wrongful detention of the foreigners. On 22 August 2020, striking down cases against thirty-four Tablighi Jamaat members, including twenty-eight foreigners detained at the Ahmednagar jail in Maharashtra, the Bombay High Court's Aurangabad bench remarked: 'A political government tries to find scapegoat when there is pandemic or calamity, and the circumstances show that there is probability that these foreigners were chosen to make them scapegoats.'[10] The court also said 'the propaganda against the so-called religious activity was unwarranted.'[11]

The ordeal of the Tablighis ended as different courts in the country let them off and the foreigners lodged in different jails in the country returned to their own countries, carrying back psychological scars that would perhaps never heal.

The Tablighis who were incarcerated have returned to their homes. Now the debate should be whether the indigenous Tablighis at AMU are benefiting the institution or harming its image as a modern, progressive university.

8

Reviving Sir Syed's Mission, and Death of a Dream

A university does not consist of just a set of buildings. Unlike a palace or a pavilion, a university is a seat of learning where ideas are debated, theories discussed and life's issues pondered upon.

We have discussed earlier how the decline of AMU began in the nineties. Its expansion, its intake of students disproportionate to its capacity to accommodate them due to the shortage of residential halls, made AMU almost unmanageable.

But there comes a moment in the life of an institution when it gets a second chance to regain its lost glory, to recover at least partially the losses suffered over the years. That moment came when a proud alumnus, former president of the AMU

Students' Union and founder of Iqra International Educational Foundation Dr Abidullah Ghazi (1936–2021), founded the Academy of South Asian Studies (ASAS) at AMU during the tenure of Mohammad Naseem Farooqui as vice chancellor (1990–1994).

Ghazi came from a family of noted Islamic scholars and freedom fighters. His great-grandfather Maulana Abdullah Ansari had set up the Sunni theology department at MAO College upon Sir Syed's invitation and had also led the prayers at Sir Syed's funeral in 1898. His grandfather Maulana Mohammed Mian Ansari was a freedom fighter and an active spirit behind the Silk Letter Movement, which had established a government-in-exile in Afghanistan to oppose the British Raj in the early twentieth century; and his father, Maulana Hamidullah Ansari Ghazi, was also a freedom fighter and a noted Urdu journalist and writer.

Abidullah Ghazi had witnessed an exciting era at AMU. After completing his MA in political science from AMU in 1959—former Vice President M. Hamid Ansari was his classmate—Abidullah Ghazi taught at Jamia's high school and Delhi college before he went to the London School of Economics (LSE), from where he did an MA in economics. He subsequently moved to Harvard to do a PhD on the revivalist views of Raja Rammohan Roy.

Among the many institutions he had attended—including Jamia Millia Islamia, where he completed his high school—Aligarh was what made Abidullah Ghazi. In his autobiography *Jahad-e-Musalsal: Aligarh Se Aligarh Tak* (Constant Struggle: From Aligarh to Aligarh), Abidullah Ghazi expresses his profuse fulsome gratitude to AMU:

I had done my education and training at different places before and after my time at Aligarh. But Aligarh was an important milestone in my educational journey. To this day I am associated with this milestone intellectually, mentally and spiritually. I found in Sir Syed's institution my intellectual, mental and educational home. It is here that I got the love of my teachers, the selfless affection of friends, and the delightful rivalry of my rivals, the eventfulness of my actions, the maturity of my ideas, the audacity to set goals and the tenderness of love. My experiences at AMU and later, its memories, turned me, a product of autumn, into an evergreen person.[1]

Few alumni of AMU loved their alma mater as Abidullah Ghazi did. He admitted that he could not have become so resilient and firm in his decisions had he not gone to AMU. Faiz Alam College in Meerut was an option for him after his matriculation, but he wrote to his father in Mumbai informing him of his wish to study at AMU. His father backed his choice, in a letter that reminded him of the roots the Ghazis had with AMU. He wrote:

Your wish to go to Aligarh is an attempt to reestablish our relationship with AMU that my grandfather Maulana Abdullah Ansari had established with Sir Syed and the Aligarh Movement. This relationship continued with my uncle Ahmad Mian, who was among the first teachers of Theology at the College, another uncle, Rashid Ahmed of the Persian department, and younger brother Mahadullah Ansari, who too studied there. Even today, my cousin sister Mahmooda Khatoon and her husband Shah Farooque Ahmed Sabri stay there. They will be your guide. Many students of your grandfather are teachers. Professor Habib (Mohammed Habib of history) was a student of my grandfather's. He had met my father in Kabul in 1936. You should seek guidance from him too. My friend Maulana Abdul Shahid Khan Sherwani will be your patron there and I am sending some money to him for your expenses. Your joining Aligarh is like completion of part of my and my father's goals. If God wants some tasks to be fulfilled, he takes help from his subjects. God wants you to do some big works in life and Aligarh is part of that plan. I may be in poor condition, but I will keep helping you.[2]

Abidullah Gazi says that at the end of the letter his father wrote a few sentences, which became the guiding principles of his life. His father wrote: 'Ignore the differences and disruptions in our clan and concentrate on educational achievements and possibilities in life. Achieve perfection in whatever you do. The real thing is perfection of the art, and degrees and certificates are mere testimonies. Acquiring them is not the goal, since they (are) the means of reaching the goal.'

Abidullah Ghazi didn't disappoint his father as he excelled in studies as well as in extracurricular activities, such as debating, writing verse and recitations, and dabbling in student politics too.

In 1983 he set up Iqra International Educational Foundation in Chicago in 1983 with the help of his educationist-wife Tasneema Ghazi, whom he had met in Aligarh while they studied there. They revolutionized Islamic teaching through their books for the new generation of Muslims in the West. Acknowledging his services in a tribute to him after his death, Bangalore-based senior journalist Maqbool Ahmed Siraj wrote:

> For migrants or new settlers, livelihood concerns are first and foremost and override all other assignments. But Dr Abidullah Ghazi thought about the next generation and invested all his time, talent, energy, insight, zeal and maybe resources, to put in place a vast library of textbooks for children to learn Islam in an ambience where rationality challenged every bit of religion, status quo and credos of faith.[3]

Abidullah Ghazi always wanted to do something for AMU, his alma mater, which had shaped his thoughts and given him the courage to fight his battles in life. Despite taking American citizenship in 1983 and subsequently becoming an Overseas Citizen of India (OCI), he kept his association with India and Aligarh intact. About his relationship with Aligarh, he says: 'My relationship with Aligarh is akin to that of parents and their son. And this relationship grows stronger as we grow older.'[4]

His sister Shahnaz and Urdu writer and brother-in-law Shams Kanwal settled in Aligarh, and his mother too went to live there after his father's death. His younger brother Arshad relocated from Saudi Arabia to Aligarh.

Ghazi wanted to utilize the experiences he had gained at Harvard for the benefit of AMU and Indian Muslims. He set up the Academy of South Asian Studies (ASAS) at Aligarh, initially running it from Muzammil Manzil and subsequently moving it to AMU Professor Iqbal Ahmed Ansari's house. Mohammed Naseem Farooqui, the VC at the time, offered him an old building near Suleiman Hall on the campus for the headquarters of ASAS. It was provided on lease for just one year. The upper floor, remembers Abidullah Ghazi, was in a dilapidated condition. He says he spent Rs 1 lakh to restore and repair it to make it functional. 'I had planned that we would hand it over to the university', says Ghazi.[5]

ASAS was registered, and the AMU vice chancellor was made the ex-officio head of the board of directors. Abidullah Ghazi became the chairman, while senior teacher Professor Masoodul Hassan became the vice-chairman and Dr Nafees Ahmed the secretary. An IT institute was also opened here, and training began with the use of twenty-five computers. Abidullah Ghazi writes that research on at least a dozen subjects began, which could have shaped the future of Indian Muslims. The main purpose of the academy, writes Ghazi, was to find new windows for a developed and respectable existence for Muslims in south Asia, especially in India. Interfaith dialogue was part of the programmes that the academy took up.

Professor Noorul Hasan Naqvi was roped in to prepare programmes for ASAS on the basis of the National Council for Educational Research and Training (NCERT) syllabus for Urdu-medium schools and madrassas. The subjects were the social sciences, science and Urdu, and books were published on these subjects.

The second project was to prepare books on leading Muslim freedom fighters, educationists and other important personalities of pre- and post-Independence India. The programme for social studies, writes Ghazi, involved the sourcing of scholars from AMU's departments of social studies, political science and economics, to research the areas in which Muslims were once pioneers. There was a plan to also study the various industries in which Muslims dominated—locks (Aligarh), scissors (Meerut), brass (Moradabad), glass (Firozabad) and stone (Rajasthan)—and find out how the infrastructure for these industries could be improved and what recommendations could be made to the government. This project, if implemented, could have proved revolutionary.

The academy had also undertaken the important work of translation of academic material. Since Iqra International Educational Trust had received an important project—preparation of the syllabus for the madrassas in Singapore from the primary to grade-ten levels in English—a number of madrassa graduates pursuing higher education at AMU were engaged in this project. The syllabus was also prepared in Urdu, and all the scholars engaged in this work were paid well.

In a way, the academy was a kind of resuscitation of the Scientific Society Sir Syed had founded in 1864. Though the purpose of the society was to translate important books published in English to Urdu, the academy had also aimed to create an atmosphere of dialogue, debate and sound research, and bring communities together through interfaith dialogues. The academy was like a revisitation of some of the works Sir Syed had started and left, as his focus turned to founding MAO College. It was an attempt to revive Sir Syed's mission.

However, like most good things, this academy too came to an end. Abidullah Ghazi didn't have the time to be present physically in Aligarh to run the show. He depended on some persons who didn't honour their commitments. The people entrusted with important responsibilities didn't take much interest in them. Ghazi felt cheated. The university also didn't do justice to the academy. The building given to the academy on lease was taken back as it was allegedly an 'encroachment'.[6]

Abidullah Ghazi said he was not even informed before the books, computers and furniture that belonged to the academy were thrown out of the building and left on the road outside.[7] He had tried to revolutionize AMU.

A very hurt Abidullah Ghazi recalls that he felt like a son deprived of his inheritance and robbed of honour and dignity. He says that no authorities contacted him, even though he had told the earlier Vice Chancellor M. Naseem Farooqui that he would hand over the building with all its possessions, like the office, books and furniture, whenever the university demanded it. But another vice chancellor was misguided by some elements at the university, and he couldn't understand the sentiments of a senior Alig for the alma mater. Though the academy received a major jolt with this dis-housing, work at the institution continued at the NGO office of a teacher, Dr Nafees Ahmed. But the soul of this academy, its spirit and enthusiasm, were damaged forever. It was the death of a dream.

Abidullah Ghazi, who would attend programmes of both the communists and an Islamic organization like the Jamaat-e-Islami Hind at AMU as a student, called himself a nationalist Muslim. He believed in the Ganga-Jamuni Tehzeeb (composite culture) of India and saw Indian Muslims' future in a pluralist, peaceful India. He studied at AMU at a time when many student leaders and his other friends had migrated to Pakistan. The student leaders who migrated to Pakistan also included an interesting character named Ahmed Saeed, nicknamed 'Anda'. A habitual disrupter, Saeed Anda often used the 'Islam in Danger' slogan in his speeches.

Abidullah Ghazi cites an interesting incident during Dr Zakir Hussain's tenure as vice chancellor. After Dr Zakir Hussain reduced the Muharram holidays, a student leader named Jaffer Mehdi Tabaan sat on a hunger strike. The Shia students and staff saw this reduction in Muharram holidays as an interference in their religious affairs. Even the Sunnis joined the Shias in their agitation. The students' union held a meeting to show their solidarity with Tabaan when his condition worsened as the hunger strike continued. Interestingly, even Dr Zakir Hussain attended this meeting. Never one to let go an opportunity to attack the administration, Saeed Anda made a speech, which had a memorable line: 'It is regrettable that in this University Zakir Hussain is stopping people from zikr-e-Hussain (commemoration of Imam Hussain, the Prophet's grandson who was martyred at the Battle of Karbala in Iraq).'[8]

But Zakir Sahab gave a fitting reply to this. He said: 'How can Zakir Hussain dare to stop commemoration of Hussain. Hussain should be commemorated every day and there is no leave required for this. More than taking leave to mourn the martyrdom of Hussain, he is better remembered by holding classes and getting an education.'[9] And then Zakir Sahab went on to give a good speech on the life of Imam Hussain before proceeding to the spot where the student leader Tabaan was on a hunger strike. He sympathized with his cause, admired his spirit and persuaded him to end the strike by offering him a glass of fruit juice.

Years later, Abidullah Ghazi met the elder brother of Ahmed Saeed 'Anda' at the Prophet's Mosque in Medina during an Umrah. The Umrah is a pilgrimage of a level lower than the Haj. While Haj is done annually, Umrah can be performed through the year. While both Haj and Umrah take place in Mecca, most pilgrims also visit Medina to pay tribute to the Prophet, who is buried there. The elder brother of Ahmed Saeed 'Anda' informed Ghazi of his brother's death back in

Pakistan. Abidullah Ghazi pays tribute to 'Anda' in glowing terms. 'No history of the students' union at AMU will be complete without Ahmed Saeed. For a long time he was the students' union and the students' union was him.'[10]

Dr Abidullah Ghazi also recalls his friendship with M. Hamid Ansari, who did his MA in political science at AMU before he was selected for the Indian Foreign Service. Dr Abidullah Ghazi and Hamid Ansari were close friends and classmates. Ghazi came from a family of religious scholars in Anbehta in Saharanpur district in Uttar Pradesh—his great-grandfather Abdullah Ansari was among the contemporaries of Sir Syed and the one whom Sir Syed had asked to set up the Deeniyat or theology department at MAO College. Hamid Ansari is a grand-nephew of the freedom fighter and former president of the Indian National Congress, Dr Mukhtar Ahmed Ansari.

Both Ghazi and Ansari shared the same perspectives on the Indian political situation in the 1950s. Both were nationalist Muslims and opposed the creation of Pakistan since they believed in a united, inclusive India with a composite culture. Since both came from families of freedom fighters, they saw themselves as inheritors of a huge legacy. However, their similarities ended there.

Their hobbies and tastes were different. While Ansari didn't take any interest in student politics, Abidullah Ghazi was miles away from cricket, which kept Ansari engaged. Ansari would be umpiring a match if he was not reading books. Ghazi writes that he never saw Ansari batting or bowling but saw him always umpiring at cricket matches. This experience on the cricket ground must have come in handy when Hamid Ansari served as vice president and chairman of the Rajya Sabha (2007–2017).

Abidullah Ghazi writes that the night before the final-year paper on 'World Constitution' for MA (political science) was to be held, he went to Hamid Ansari's room to 'bore him'.[11] He saw that Ansari was in his bed reading a book titled *House of Lords*. Since Ghazi was preparing for the World Constitution paper and had not found anything on the House of Lords in the British Constitution section of the syllabus, he began to panic. He says he was not surprised to see Hamid Ansari reading a huge book because he always read original texts and never depended on notes. Ghazi was worried that he had not read this chapter on the House of Lords at all. He asked Ansari if he was reading it for the exam, and Ansari replied asking what else would people read on the night before an exam.

Abidullah asked Ansari if he knew that there was going to be a question on the House of Lords in the paper, and Ansari said yes, as a teacher had called it 'important'. Ghazi became worried and told Ansari to give him the book once he had read it.

Ghazi returned to his room and began preparing for 'important' questions. After a while, Ansari came to Ghazi's room and put that book on the table, telling Ghazi to read it.

After an hour or so, Ghazi opened the book that Ansari had given him earlier that night. The book had nothing to do with the House of Lords in the British Parliament but was actually about Lord's, the famous cricket ground in England, and had interesting anecdotes from the matches held there. Abidullah was angry and went to Ansari's room. He threw the book on Ansari, who was asleep. 'What is this joke?' Ghazi asked. 'What happened?' asked Ansari. 'Are you reading about cricket even on the night before the exam?' asked Ghazi. Ansari said he always stopped reading on a subject a week before exams and read only about cricket just before the exam.[12]

When the results came, both Ansari and Ghazi passed with flying colours. However, the topper was Shahzad Ahmed who, according to Ghazi, became a teacher of political science in the US. Ansari became an IFS officer and later vice president of India and chairman of the Rajya Sabha, while Ghazi settled in the US, doing excellent work through the Iqra International Education Foundation.

Ghazi tells us that the credit for their success goes to Aligarh, which developed leadership qualities in students who then went on to excel in whatever fields they later chose for themselves.

July 1958 to May 1959 was the most crucial period of his life, says Abidullah Ghazi, and these years were spent on the AMU campus. It is during this period that he cleared his MA finals in political science. Many other doors opened for him. He was elected the students' union president unopposed and also became the first president of the National Council of University Students of India (NCUSI). Students associated with the Students' Federation of India (SFI), the student wing of the communists, and the JIH, backed Abidullah Ghazi's candidature for the students' union president's post at Aligarh. He knew the members of the JIH's pioneer members at AMU, like Nijatullah Siddiqui, Ashfaque Ahmed, Dr Abdul Haque Ansari and Irfan Ahmed Khan.

Abidullah Ghazi's neigbhours in the AMU hostel were interesting people—Nijatullah Siddiqui, M. Hamid Ansari and Desh Raj. Nijatullah Siddiqui was a propagator of JIH's views. Desh Raj was from Bulandshahr in UP and used a lot of expletives when he spoke, but his expletives were colourful and 'acceptable'.

Ghazi tells us that initially he was reluctant to contest the union elections, but when his friends, both in the Jamaat-e-Islami Hind and the leftists, pressured him to, he agreed, but on the condition that he should be elected unopposed. Ghazi says that in the history of the students' union at AMU till then, only once had a candidate, Khwaja Ghulam Us Saiyiden, won the post unopposed. But when Abidullah Ghazi's nomination papers were filed, he saw that two more nominations had been done. One was of Umar Farooque, a close friend of Ghazi, who reasoned that election was a tradition at Aligarh and he would not allow Abidullah Ghazi to win unopposed. The second candidate was Ibn Farid from the JIH, a known Urdu writer. Ghazi saw in this situation a good excuse to withdraw his nomination, as the election was no longer unopposed. However, his friends didn't allow him to. But here we must detour briefly and look at the circumstances in which Abidullah Ghazi had resumed his studies after he spent a year at the Tambram Sanatorium in Tamil Nadu.

After he completed his graduation, a doctor had diagnosed Ghazi with tuberculosis (TB) and had advised him recuperation at a sanitorium at Tambram in Tamil Nadu, where he spent many months. His family's financial condition was bad, as his father's income as a journalist and writer in Bombay (now Mumbai), was quite meagre. The family had moved from Bijnor to Bombay in the early 1950s. Ghazi wanted to help his father who was struggling to run the Urdu weekly *Jamhuriat* (Republic) he owned in Bombay.

Ghazi informs us that on his return from Tambram he wanted to help his father at his newspaper. 'The family lived in one room in a building on Mohammed Ali Road,' recalls Salman Ghazi, Abidullah Ghazi's younger brother, who runs Iqra International Education Foundation in Mumbai. Salman runs it along with his activist-wife Uzma Naheed.

Since the room was too small to accommodate yet another member, his father put up Abidullah Ghazi at a friend's. He stayed in a Mullaji's room in Wazir Building at Bhendi Bazaar. Mullaji had a sweets shop and would use the room to make mithai during the day. By night, homeless people like Ghazi and many others slept there. Ghazi writes that the bedbugs would attack them every night but most of the occupants in the room were so tired that they would not even realize it.

As his father and two younger brothers, Tariq and Khalid, were out of Mumbai on some work for weeks together, he took over the weekly. Running up and down four floors in the rains of Mumbai, visiting the press and sending the paper to subscribers and distributors by post constituted hard work, but he endured it. Yet he didn't fall ill. This proved that he had been cured of his TB.

Meanwhile, he received a letter from his uncle Mahamadullah Ansari Ghazi from Afghanistan, saying that he had a confirmed job for him in the education department of the Afghanistan government. Since Abidullah Ghazi had ancestral properties in Afghanistan, his uncle asked him to go over with a power of attorney from his father Maulana Hamidullah Ansari Ghazi. Abidullah Ghazi was all set to go and had got his passport ready, but he had no money that was needed for the travel. His father was neck-deep in debt. He wrote to an uncle, Khalil, in Jaunpur, who was a zamindar, seeking Rs 50 as an interest-free loan. He had earlier met this uncle in Aligarh. The uncle sent him Rs 250.

Clutching his passport and the letter from his uncle in Afghanistan, Abidullah Ghazi approached the Afghanistan embassy in Delhi. Looking at his file, the officer asked him if he had a BT (bachelor's in teaching) or BEd (bachelor's in education) degree. He told the officer that he was a BA (Hons) in English with a first-class degree from AMU. But the officer said that a B.Ed degree was a must for the teaching job he had received an offer for and refused him a visa.

With his hopes of going to Afghanistan dashed, Abidullah didn't know what to do next. He felt he could not go back to Mumbai, given the conditions in which his father and siblings were living. Going to Anbehta and Deoband, where some relatives still lived, didn't look attractive.

Though he had no money to see him through AMU, he still travelled to Aligarh through Delhi. He says he went there to say goodbye to his friends and teachers. Seeing him there, everyone was excited. Though Dr Zakir Hussain had quit as VC, he had spoken very highly of Abidullah to his successor Syed Bashir Hussain Zaidi. Zakir Sahab wanted to deposit some money for Abidullah Ghazi's studies for his MA, but the pro-vice chancellor, the younger brother of Zakir Hussain, Yusuf Hussain Khan, told Abidullah Ghazi that he would pay him Rs 20 per month. His stay and food at the hostel were made free, and a Sudanese friend, Bahauddin Syed Umar, even auctioned his wristwatch to pay for Abidullah's admission to the MA course.

Despite his popularity on the campus, Ghazi didn't want to fight the elections as his priority was his studies and clearing the MA exam. He saw in it a guarantee to his bright future. But his friends insisted that he fight the elections. Meanwhile, both Ibn Farid and Umar Farooque withdrew their candidatures, paving the way for the election of Ghazi as the unopposed students' union president. His inaugural speech as the union president was very impressive. He had said:

> Muslims have a great future in India and Aligarh is a successful laboratory of Hindu-Muslim unity. Muslims should not get depressed and should not leave the country. Our future is neither linked with the Islamic world nor with Pakistan; our future lies with Hindus and Hindustan. The secular democratic system of India is the best in the world and to make it work Muslims don't need to establish a separate political party. They need to work with other secular parties. Aligarh is a laboratory of Hindu-Muslim unity and we have to make it successful.[13]

This speech was carried by the press and talked about a lot. Since there were still a few elements at AMU who sympathized with the Muslim League, Abidullah Ghazi, as the union president, wanted to send a message to them too. His views were in tune with what leaders of the nationalist Jamiat Ulama-i-Hind like Maulana Abul Kalam Azad, Maulana Hussain Ahmed Madni and Maulana Hifzur Rahman had said earlier. These leaders had opposed the two-nation theory of the Muslim League and wanted Muslims to not get seduced by Jinnah's promise of a new country. Abidullah Ghazi had imbibed the values these great Muslim leaders stood for. The Jamiat Ulama-i-Hind, founded in 1919, had abstained from participating in elections. And its leaders were happy to get a few Rajya Sabha nominations from the Congress party. (However, currently even this tokenism from Congress to the Jamiat leaders is invisible; there has not been a single Jamiat leader in the Rajya Sabha for half a decade.)

While Abidullah Ghazi was still the union president at AMU, students from different universities in the country decided to form the National Council of University Students of India (NCUSI). Ghazi participated in its inaugural function in Delhi and delivered a powerful speech on Indian democracy, on south Asia and the Islamic world's relationship with India. It was appreciated, and Ghazi was elected vice president of the NCUSI. Since a student of Osmania University, Hyderabad, was elected as its president but didn't accept the post, Abidullah Ghazi was elected as the first president of this all-India student organization. This was a great honour for him and for AMU too. He worked closely with the Delhi University student leader, Jyoti Shankar Singh. Ghazi got ample opportunities to put across his views on behalf of AMU, and to an extent on behalf of the Muslims of India, from a national platform. It is through this association with NCUSI that he came in contact with Prime Minister Jawaharlal Nehru, President Rajendra Prasad, University Grants Commission's Chairman C.D. Deshmukh, Education Secretary Humayun Kabir, Deputy Secretary of Education Khwaja Ghulam Us Saiyidain and many other luminaries.

As a student, Abidullah Ghazi suffered greatly on account of his poor financial condition. He didn't have the money to pay for even a round trip to Delhi. He narrates an incident that illustrates his patience and resilience. He was eligible to get Rs 20 in monthly allowance from the students' union, but he never took it. Once, he went to Delhi to attend a meeting of the NCUSI and had no money to buy a train ticket back to Aligarh.

He needed just Rs 3. He was the Aligarh representative of *Aina* (Mirror), an organ of Shama Publications in Delhi. He visited its office as some money was due to him from the magazine. Its editor was famous writer Zoe Ansari, a friend of his father's.

He met Zoe Ansari with great expectations but was disappointed when Ansari said he couldn't give him any money because the magazine was struggling and would close soon.

From Zoa Ansari's office, Ghazi took a bus and went to meet his friend and ICS officer Saad Mahmood Hashmi. Hashmi met him warmly but said he was in hurry as he had to rush for a meeting. He gave Ghazi a lift in his car and dropped him outside the Red Fort. Ghazi could not summon up the courage to borrow money from this prosperous friend. Neither had the friend asked him if he needed any help.

Ghazi walked down to the historic Jama Masjid area, sat on its stone steps and began to think about what he could do now. His aunt (father's sister) Maimoona lived nearby, and he began to trace his steps towards her house when on the way he remembered his father's friend Anwar Sabri who too lived nearby. He called on Chacha Anwar Sabri, who was very courteous. After he offered Ghazi a good lunch and tea, Ghazi hesitatingly asked him: 'Uncle, I have to say something.' 'Yes son, go ahead,' said the uncle. 'I need Rs 3 for my travel to Aligarh.' This uncle gave him Rs 20, even though Ghazi had demanded just Rs 3. With the extra money Ghazi bought sweets for his aunt Maimuna and even saved some for a party with friends at Aligarh.

After completing his MA, Abidullah Ghazi became a schoolteacher at Jamia's high school in Delhi and would receive Rs 260 monthly. Out of this, he says, he kept only Rs 40 for himself while he sent the rest to his mother in Bombay. After a year he taught at Delhi College (it later became Dr Zakir Hussain Delhi College) before he won a scholarship to study at the London School of Economics and later another scholarship to study at Harvard. The boy who once didn't have Rs 3 to buy a train ticket from Delhi to Aligarh became a famous scholar and the toast of meetings and workshops, even as he penned over 150 books to enable Muslim children growing up in the west to understand Islam.

The fascinating journey of Dr Abidullah Ghazi ended on 11 April 2021 when he died in Chicago. In a long poem, 'Yaad-e-Aligarh' (Memories of Aligarh), Ghazi had recounted his days on the campus:

Muqabil mein aaye jasarat thi kisko
Koi rok de badh ke himmat thi kisko
Pukare koi humko taqat thi kisko
Nigahein milane ki jurat thi kisko
Ke har bul lhawas ko the hum taziyana
Bahut yaad aata hai guzra zamana

(No one had courage to face us
No one had temerity to stop us
No one had the strength to challenge us
No one could see eye-to-eye to us
We were a whip to every avaricious person
I remember the days gone by).

9

Bastion of Liberalism or Hotbed of Islamism?

WHEN I called up a senior professor at AMU to get his perspective on the growing Islamism at the university, he sagely advised me not to write about it. His concern was more about how it might be construed by the outside world than about corrosion of the liberal, scientific, progressive values the campus has suffered in its efforts to make Muslims 'better Muslims'.

Many senior teachers on the campus, serving and retired, and alumni living outside Aligarh admit the growing influence of a religious organization like the Jamaat-e-Islami Hind on the campus but prefer not to talk about it publicly. But sweeping an issue under the carpet or discussing it only behind closed doors does not make it disappear. As someone who immensely benefited from AMU's intellectual ferment and its vibrant atmosphere in the mid 1980s, this writer is dismayed at the way the Islamic group is occupying the space being vacated by liberals on the campus.

The Jamaat-E-Islami Hind, and later its student wings— SIMI, now banned, and SIO—took root in AMU and spread their tentacles even as the liberals got sidelined to such an extent that they are on the periphery today.

Though JIH was founded on 26 August 1941 in Lahore by an Islamic scholar, Sayyid Abul Ala Maududi, the students of AMU had been attracted to Maududi's thoughts since the mid-1930s. The core of Maududi's thoughts is that Islam is a complete way of life. According to him, Islam expects its adherents not to confine themselves to merely performing the rituals of shahda—the declaration that God is one and Muhammad is His Prophet—namaz—fasting during Ramzan— Haj and zakat—the giving away of 2.5 per cent of one's annual savings to charity). Islamic scholar Dr Farida Khanum sums up Maulana Maududi's teaching succinctly:

> The core of Maulana Maududi's teachings is that Islam is a complete way of life. It is not just concerned with an individual's life. It impacts the collective life of humans in all areas, including economic, political, cultural, national and international. Islam came to this world to overpower other systems and it is duty of Muslims to establish Hukumat-e-Illahia or rule of God on earth. It is duty of Muslims to struggle and establish Islamic rule wherever they get a chance.[1]

Don't we smell pan-Islamism here? The spiritual aspect of Islam suggests that a Muslim's duty is merely to take the message of the Quran and Sunnah, or traditions of the Prophet, to people through peaceful means. No one is ordained to force Islam down the throats of people of another faith.

The main objective of JIH is Iqaamat-e-Deen or establishment of the Islamic way of life.

> The doors of the organization are thrown open to any citizen who accepts the sacred motto *La ilaha illallah, Muhammadur Rasulullah* (the Divine Being is solely Allah, there being no God except Him, and Muhammad is Allah's messenger) in its entirety and all its implications, and is ready to work for the establishment of the divine order in the land. It rejects the un-Islamic principle 'the end justifies the means'; instead, the Islamic movement professes the way adopted by the prophets, the way of peaceful and non-violent transmission of ideas.[2]

Because of the propagation of political Islam that he and his followers did, General Zia-ul-Haq is believed to have 'Islamized' Pakistan under the influence of Maududi's teachings.

Much before Aurangabad (India)-born Maulana Maududi established the Jamaat-e-Islami Hind, he launched the monthly magazine *Tarjumanul Quran* in 1933. This magazine became the vehicle for his thoughts and ideas, which reached a sizeable section of educated Muslims in the country. In the 1930s, AMU was a bastion of communists, and students and teachers aligned with leftist ideas dominated the scene before the Muslim League injected the diabolical two-nation theory into the university and weaned away a sizeable section of the student community. Aligarh provided a conducive atmosphere to students who upheld progressive and liberal ideas, and many of them went on to become noted poets and writers. The liberal, left-leaning students at AMU in those days included Khwaja Ahmed Abbas, Hayatullah Ansari, Asrarul Haq Majaz, Ali Sardar Jafri, Akhtarul Imaan, Moin Ahsan Jazbi and Akhtar Raipuri.

In his research paper, Noman Badar Falahi, an Arabic scholar at AMU, details the genesis of Maulana Maududi's popularity in Aligarh. *Tarjumanul Quran*, says Falahi, carried essays that were distributed among students at AMU as part of a campaign to stop the increasing 'godlessness' among them.

> (Volunteers of) Lahore's Seerat Committee and Muslim League would distribute Maulana Maududi's literature free among Aligarh students. A remarkable change came about in the thought process of the students. A circle of students believing in Maududi's postulation of Islam being a way of life got created. They finally began organizing themselves in 1936 and subsequently established a Darul Mutalla or Library at a room rented by Abdullah Safdar Ali at Shamshad Market (near the AMU campus). It later came to be known as Islamic Library.[3]

Falahi refers to the comments and observations by many senior teachers at AMU like Prof. Asloob Ahmed Ansari, Prof. Ahmed Soorti and Prof. Reyazur Rahman Sherwani, which testify that the Islamic movement among AMU students had begun in the mid 1930s. An 'Islamic Week', aimed at creating interest among students in Islam, was also held annually. It is during this week that Maulana Maududi was invited to give his first lecture at Strachey Hall in 1940. Maududi's series of articles in *Tarjumanul Quran* on 'Political Struggle' had already endeared him to a section of Muslim youths. He already had a fan following on the campus, which many of this flock rued was turning godless as the communists had an upper hand there. Noman Badar Falahi quotes Mubarak Ali Khan, an AMU student in the 1940s, as saying:

> It was towards the end of 1940. The University was preparing for the Islamic Week and Dr Ameer Hasan Siddiqui was main force behind the programme. Maulana Maududi was one of the invitees for the programme. We were aware of the Maulana's writings through *Tarjumanul Quran* for the last three-four years. The union library would subscribe to this magazine and it would attract the attention of teachers and students. It attracted many people after the series on political struggle began appearing in it. Maulana Maududi's fascinating style of writing, balanced and strong arguments, not only attracted the youths but elders too, and everyone was glad about Maulana Maududi's visit and wanted to meet him.[4]

AMU then was intellectually vibrant and the students looked forward to hearing Maulana Maududi. Maududi's lecture *'Islami hukumat kis tarah qayam hoti hai'* (How is Islamic rule established) was heard in pin-drop silence and, without naming the Muslim League, the Khaksar Tehrik or Movement (the revolutionary Allama Mashraqi had begun this anti-British movement, which opposed the partition of India and laid stress on Hindu–Muslim unity), Maududi criticized them for their actions. Interestingly, it was Professor Habib, leader of the communist lobby and then head of the department of history and politics, who presided at this function. 'When are you going to give us an opportunity to hear you again?' asked Habib.[5] This open liking of Maulana Maududi's speech by Prof. Habib gave a shot in the arm to Islamists on the campus. Prof. Habib also hosted Maulana Maududi at his house in Badar Bagh in Aligarh for a night. Prof. Habib's son, eminent historian and Professor Emeritus at AMU Irfan Habib, observed in an interview: 'I remember that I was a schoolboy and Maulana Maududi came to our house and stayed at night. There was a difference between my parents over his stay here. My mother didn't like it that the Maulana stayed here but my father said that he was a guest.'[6]

In the same 'Islamic Week', several other leading scholars of Islam, like Syed Sulaiman Nadvi, Maulana Abdul Majid Daryabadi, Qari Mohammaed Tayyab and Maulana Aslam Jairajpuri would visit the campus and deliver lectures. Having worked tirelessly to attract students to propagate the 'Islamic way of life', the movement began to bear fruit. In the 1940s, the prominent students who were part of the 'Islamic Circle' at AMU included Afzal Hussain, Abdul Azeem Khan, Rao Shamshad Ali Khan, Aasi Ziyaee, Abdullah Safdar Ali, Shamsul Hoda, Syed Hussain, Saeed Ahmed, Farogh Ahmed, Ahmed Soorti, Rahmatullah Shah and Syed Zainul Abideen.[7]

The irony was that the students and teachers at AMU might have come under the spell of Maulana Maududi, but the AMU founder Sir Syed didn't pass the 'Islamic' test that Maududi put him to. Maududi blamed Sir Syed for distorting the temperament of Muslims in India post 1857. Reviewing the PhD thesis titled '*Mujadid Alf Saani Ka Tasawur Tauheed*' by Dr Burhan Ahmed Farooqui, a former student of AMU, Maududi wrote in his magazine *Tarjamanul Quran*: 'The fact is that whatever unruliness or stubbornness that came among Muslims, it traces directly or indirectly to Sir Syed. He was the leader of renewal on this land and left the world after spoiling the temperament of the entire quom or community.'[8]

Partition hit the Islamic Movement of the Jamaat-e-Islami Hind too. After Partition, the JIH split into three, one splinter each in India, Pakistan and Bangladesh. The Jamaat-e-Islami Hind was formally launched at a meeting in April 1948 at Allahabad.[9] Many leading lights of the Islamic Movement at AMU, both students and teachers, migrated to Pakistan as they hoped they would get to implement their ideas in a country created in the name of Islam. That hope has remained unfulfilled till date.

The Islamic Library at Shamshad Market remained the markaz, or centre, for the students belonging to the Islamic Movement. These students began asserting themselves and even fielded their candidates in the students' union elections at AMU. In the 1950s, the students at the campus who were under the influence of JIH ideology included Nijatullah Siddiqui, Abdul Haq Ansari, Fazlur Rahman Faridi, Hamidullah Ibn Farid, Syed Anwar Ali, Iqbal Ahmed Ansari and Anwar Siddiqui.

Dr Abidullah Ghazi, who spent eight years (1951–1959) at Aligarh and whom we discussed in detail in the previous chapter, writes in his book *Jahde Musalsal* that in the early 1950s, the AMU student community was divided into three camps—the left, the Jamaat-e-Islami and the nationalist group. The prominent leader of the last camp was Hashim Kidwai, who taught political science at AMU and later became a Rajya Sabha member. Abidullah Ghazi says that the Youth Congress, the youth wing of the Indian National Congress, was also present on campus but didn't have much influence.[10] Tariq Hasan, in his book *The Aligarh Movement and the Making of the Indian Muslim Mind 1857–2002*, quotes from Abidullah Ghazi's interview given to writer Masood Haider. In this interview, Ghazi refers to the role Jamaat-e-Islami played in those days:

> Jamaat-e-Islami in 1951 was a very small group led by Mirza Anwar Ali Beg. It had very few literary and religious activities. I did participate in many of its activities but there were not more than a dozen male students participating at one time. It was committed to Maulana Maududi's philosophy of establishing an Islamic state (later changed to Iqamat-i-Din, establishment of the religion of Islam) and not cooperating with the Indian government on any issue as it represented a Nizam-i-Batil (System of Falsehood). By siding on some community issues with the majority of Muslims, Jamaat could get some mileage, but for their own programmes they had hardly any popular support.[11]

The leftists would attend the functions of their literary group called Taraqqi Pasand Musanafeen, or Progressive Writers' Group, while the Islamists had their own Adab-e-Islami, a platform for writers and poets.

The students associated with the Islamic Library at Shamshad Market established the Students' Islamic Organization Aligarh (SIO Aligarh), in 1956. Falahi writes in a panegyrical tone that SIO Aligarh had organized Islam-loving students in the university for the first time. Members of the party began participating in the students' union elections very enthusiastically. In 1956, SIO Aligarh member Syed Ziaul Hasan Hashmi became the president, and in 1958 another member, Saghir Ahmed Bedar, became the secretary of the union. In the 1970s, this organization became very active in the university and began organizing many programmes. A big event was the symposium held on 17 September 1972 titled 'How to create an Islamic atmosphere at Muslim University'.[12] The fact that such a symposium had many takers is proof enough that the Islamic group had dug its heels in a bit deep at AMU.

Gradually, Islamic fundamentalism was injected into the minds of its members, so much so that they became rigid and assertive and began opposing liberal and progressive ideas on the campus openly. One example is the protest in 1975 it organized against the screening of a feature film by the University Film Club at the Kennedy Auditorium. Falahi says that on 30 January 1975, the Shura, or council of members, of SIO Aligarh met then vice chancellor Prof. A.M. Khusro and complained against the screening of movies featuring obscene or vulgar scenes. Subsequently, several protest letters were written to the VC objecting to the spreading of obscenity in the name of culture.[13] A three-member censor board was set up to see the films and then approve them for screening. And it was also decided that instead of feature films, educative and informative documentaries would be shown. Meanwhile, the head of the department of Sunni theology, Maulana Taqi Ameeni, began using his Friday sermons to denounce the screening of allegedly obscene films on the campus in the name of popular culture.

This writer remembers an incident from the mid 1980s, which shows how bold and confident the Islamic group had become at AMU by that decade, even as the liberals were taking a back seat. An inter-university youth festival was being held at Kennedy Auditorium. Teams from several universities were participating in the festival. Since many female students from other universities were part of the dance and drama shows at the event, the Islamic group didn't like it. Right in the middle of a show, a group of slogan-shouting boys gatecrashed into the auditorium. They threw the furniture around and shouted at the organizers, demanding a stop to the 'vulgar' show.[14] These Islamists forgot that decades ago the university founder Sir Syed had worn anklets on his old feet to dance at the annual Aligarh exhibition, seeking funds for the college that turned into AMU in 1920.

A big milestone in the life of SIO Aligarh, according to Falahi, was when the Jamaat-e-Islami leader from Jammu and Kashmir, Syed Ali Shah Geelani, addressed the annual conference of the organization. Students representing several Islamic organizations across the country had participated in this conference. In his ninety-minute speech, Geelani had said:

Islam is a burning lamp like the sun. The sun sets in one part of the world and rises in another but Islam keeps giving light without a break. But those unfortunates who have shut their eyes and ears cannot benefit from this light. The religion of Islam is like a running river and its waters never get stagnant as it is continuously flowing. Islam is also a universal religion ...We have to bring in a change. We have to change the system and the people who run the system and then only Islam can get its rightful place in this country.[15]

The Islamic Movement not only reached out to the male youth but also to the girls and some children too. The meetings of girl students associated with the Islamic movement began in 1975, and books and literature began to be sent to them in their hostel rooms.

Post Partition, the Jamaat-e-Islami Hind abandoned the pan-Islamism postulated by Maududi. Former diplomat Talmiz Ahmad observes:

> The Jamaat leaders soon realized that their theoretical postulates were out of place in India and out of harmony with the rapid change taking place internationally. They had to take a fresh look at Maududi's idea and examine his legacy. At first there was ambivalence in some quarters and serious misgivings in others. But the final verdict was in favour of democracy and secularism. 'In the present circumstances,' an official publication in 1970 declared, 'the Jamaat-e-Islami-e-Hind want that, in contrast to other totalitarian and fascist modes of government, the secular democratic mode of Government in India should endure.' The Jamaat continues to uphold this position.[16]

Initially, the JIH had been against participation in elections as it didn't have much liking for the democratic process; it wanted to establish Hukumat-e-Illahiya, or rule of God, on earth. On 18 April 2011, the JIH-backed Welfare Party of India (WPI) was launched in Delhi with many of the Jamaat functionaries holding top posts in the political party. The party's functionaries included a Christian priest too.

After Indira Gandhi declared Emergency on 25 June 1975, along with many other organizations the Jamaat-e-Islami Hind too was banned and many of its leaders arrested. However, students associated with the Jamaat and its different wings met at the common room of Habib Hall at AMU on 9 and 10 March 1976 and floated an all-India organization for Muslim students. The organization was not named at the time. After twenty-one months, the Emergency was ended on 21 March 1977, and with this even the Islamic Library at the Shamshad Market that was locked during the Emergency was unlocked on 4 April 1977 and resumed its functioning.

Post-Emergency, on 24 April 1977, the students' organization formed in March 1976 met at the Strachey Hall of AMU and named this all-India organization Students' Islamic Movement of India. Next day, a three-member (Mohammed Rafat, P. Koya, Zaki Kirmani) constitution committee presented the draft constitution for SIMI, which was accepted with minor changes.'[17]

Ahmadullah Siddiqui, a research scholar in the physics department, became its first president, and Mohammed Mumtaz Ali, a research scholar in the political science department, became its secretary. Much before SIMI deviated from its original objectives and began radicalizing Muslim youths—it has been banned since 2001—its first president, Ahmadullah Siddiqui, had talked about its purpose in an interview:

The biggest motive was to make the directionless Muslim students who were becoming morally delinquent responsible. No real work had been done among the students even after 20, 22, 24 years. There was a huge void in the Islamic movement and no genuine efforts were made to fill that void. Students and youths came forward. SIMI fulfilled this need to a great extent. SIMI got its goals fulfilled as the Islamic movement got introduced among students and youths across the country and the students became emotional and found a purpose in life.[18]

If we look at the first circular released by SIMI's Founding Secretary Mumtaz Ali soon after its formation, we don't get any hint that this organization would one day preach extremism. Its first circular released to the members reads like the agenda of an organization committed to social causes:

1. Coaching classes should be started for both students of Hindu and Muslim communities.
2. Non-Muslims should be invited over tea once in a while and dialogues should be initiated.
3. Non-Muslims should also be invited in programmes where common issues are to be discussed and we should also participate in their programmes.
4. Every unit should strive to propagate education as much as possible.
5. Efforts should be made to make associates. In this regard suggestions can be sought from secretary Mumtaz Ali.
6. Every unit should include the following features:
A. Monthly assessment training meeting

B. At least two meetings monthly to invite people to faith

C. Study from a set of basic literature

D. Sending monthly reports to the Centre from every unit

7. Every local unit or individual member can set up Baitul Maal (collective fund) and must send 10% of the monthly income to the Centre. The following things must be kept in mind:

A. A data on income and expenditure in the Baitul Maal must be kept

B. Help should be taken from the members, associates, sympathisers and those who like our works

C. All member, associate members, sympathisers must contribute something to the Baitul Maal.[19]

If these were the noble causes for which this organization was created, it is not surprising then that so many youths in the country got attracted to it. Though its headquarters were shifted to Delhi, Aligarh could never wash away the fact that SIMI, now a banned terrorist organization, came out of the womb of AMU. Maulana Saud Alam Qasmi, dean of the faculty of theology at AMU, doesn't see it unnatural or illogical that an Islamic movement got support here. 'A university is a place where different ideas grow. All these movements tried to bring discipline among students. They saved young generations from going astray in their pursuit of needless hobbies. They get a sense of social service and co-operation quite early in life,' says Qasmi, who is also editor of *Tahzib-ul-Akhlaq*, the journal Sir Syed had started for bringing about reform in Muslim society.

The Jamaat-e-Islami Hind gave its moral support to its student wing SIMI initially, but when it saw that the SIMI members had got radicalized and were turning extremist, JIH began distancing itself from it.

> Differences between SIMI and JIH cropped up and the Delhi visit of Yasser Arafat in 1981 led to further distancing. The young SIMI activists showed black flags to Arafat who was a 'Western stooge' for them in contrast to JIH for whom he was a prominent leader fighting for the Palestinians.[20]

Post-Babri Mosque demolitions in 1992:

> ... posters with pictures of the mosque, with its dome dripping blood, appeared in Muslim pockets. Some JI (Jamaat-e-Islami) members tried to dissuade SIMI from radicalising Muslim youths, but in vain. Finally, in the late 1990s the JI, its members claimed, completely distanced itself from SIMI and its activities.[21]

The SIMI doctrine sought to establish a society which is run by the Islamic principles of Shariah. The SIMI members believed that degradation in society had set in due to the faithfuls' blind following of the West. The organization members also strove to avenge the injustices done to Muslims in the communal riots in the aftermath of the Babri Mosque demolition on 6 December 1992 in Ayodhya.

> Throughout the nineteen eighties, SIMI also maintained a low profile at AMU and other parts of the country.

The demolition of the Babri Mosque in December 1992 however gave it a fresh lease of life. Even then the organization did not have more than twenty to thirty active members at Aligarh and it decided to shift its headquarters from Aligarh to New Delhi. Thus, the demolition of the Babri Mosque helped SIMI in establishing a foothold in different parts of the country.[22]

An *Indian Express* report explained the reason for the ban on SIMI:

Due to the alleged involvement of SIMI members in several terror cases in the country, a ban was imposed on the organisation in 2001 under the Prevention of Terrorism Act (POTA). SIMI was declared an unlawful group under section 3 of the Unlawful Activities Prevention Act (UAPA), 1963.

The ban on SIMI was extended periodically, except in 2008 when it was lifted following orders by a special tribunal presided by Justice Geeta Mittal. But the ban was imposed again by the Supreme Court on August 6, 2008, on the grounds of national security.

The five-year ban imposed on SIMI in 2014 came to (an) end on January 31 this year. The central government then issued a notification extending the ban on SIMI for a period of five more years starting February 1, 2019, under the UAPA. While extending the ban, the Home Ministry listed, in the notification, as many as 58 cases in which members allegedly belonging to SIMI were involved.[23]

Even before the Jamaat-e-Islami Hind broke all ties with SIMI, which had become aggressive in raising grievances after the demolition of the Babri Masjid, the Students' Islamic Organization (not to be confused with SIO Aligarh, which got dissolved into SIMI in 1977 at Aligarh) was launched in 1982 in Delhi. It was the new student wing of the JIH. 'Our main work on the campus is to assist the students in admission, their studies, and making them aware of the purpose of this life from the Islamic perspective,' says Talha Mannan, currently president of SIO at AMU. Mannan says that at the weekly meeting of the organization, issues concerning students are discussed; the emphasis is on their living a vice-free life. About participation of SIO members in elections—there are fifty SIO members at AMU—he says SIO members do participate in the students' union elections. 'The last time we had a member reaching the top in the students' union hierarchy was Abdullah Azam, who became the president in 2014. We always have some of our members in the cabinet in the union,' says Mannan.

10

To the Students of AMU

Eternal life without a sense of purpose is death
This worldly life is different; Man's striving is unique
                                    —Allama Iqbal

ALLAMA Iqbal, an admirer of Sir Syed and his movement, penned this couplet for the poem '*Talba-e-Aligarh College Ke Naam*' (Dedicated to the Students of Aligarh College) in 1907. A lot has changed on Sir Syed's expansive, leafy campus since Iqbal communicated with the students of Aligarh through this beautiful poem.

It has been seventy-four years since India threw away its colonial masters. Like the rest of the country, Aligarh too has expanded exponentially since 1907 when Iqbal penned his poem to AMU. The college was then confined mainly within the quadrangle that its founder Sir Syed himself had conceptualized and begun building on. Were Sir Syed to return to his beloved campus, he would not recognize it today—and not for its physical changes alone.

So, Iqbal wrote this poem at a juncture when a lot had already happened at MAO College—which became AMU in 1920—and in India at large. After Sir Syed's death in 1898, there was growing restlessness and discomfort among the nationalist students against their English teachers at the college. Bengal had been divided in 1905, and a year later, in 1906, the Muslim League had been established. The same League would in time fight for and get a new homeland for a chunk of Muslims on the subcontinent. But more Muslims were left behind in India in 1947 than there were in the new country. This new country of Muslims got divided in 1971, and Bangladesh was born.

The freedom struggle had picked up momentum even as animosity against the British, including the English teachers at MAO College, grew. Though Iqbal backed man's efforts for emancipation from all sorts of slavery with his stirring poetry, he did not want the boys of MAO College to demand the removal of good British teachers. Throwing out the baby with the bathwater was not prudent then, and is not prudent now.

Since there was a shortage of good educational institutions for Indians, especially Muslims, where they could gain knowledge in an atmosphere conducive to their religious and cultural traditions, MAO College was the best that Muslim youths from the late nineteenth to the late twentieth centuries could get. In his inimitable style, part prophetic, part philosophical, Iqbal encapsulates Sir Syed's vision, his dream, and also underlines the importance of hard work. Countless commentators have tried to understand the message in Iqbal's much-feted poem addressed to the boys of Aligarh. One commentator writes:

The poem, an endorsement of Sir Syed's position with regard to uplift of the Muslim society concedes to Sir Syed's opinion that India did not offer alternative education system which could compete with the western system of education, hence it must be adopted as long as it is need to be, to allow the youth of the community to grow and become mature. It highlights the importance of hard work and continuous and concerted effort as the only way forward.[1]

Iqbal dedicated a poem to Sir Syed too. And this too has been talked about a lot. *Syed ki Lauh-E-Turbat* (The Gravestone of Syed) is a monologue that Iqbal wrote as if Sir Syed himself were speaking. Adopting the persona of Sir Syed, Iqbal addresses important members of the society, including leaders, teachers, students and religious scholars. A couplet in the poem is a clarion call to all: '*Sonewalon ko jaga de shair ke aijaz se/Kharmane batil jala de shoala-e-awaz se* (Awaken the somnolent with your stirring verses/Vanquish falsehood with the charm of your voice).

One hundred and fourteen years after Iqbal dedicated his poem to students of MAO College and a century after the college became a university, his lines still carry uncanny resonance and relevance. Visit the Victoria Gate, the historic Strachey Hall or the white-domed massive Jama Masjid—all at the quadrangle created in Sir Syed's lifetime as part of the MAO College campus—you will hear red stones and bricks speak to you in whispers: don't let us down. Move to the jali or the iron grill guarding the open-to-the-skies, green grass-laden grave of Sir Syed at the masjid's premises and lend your ears to hear the voice of the old man of Aligarh. He is calling out to the community, especially to the students at the campus. He seems to be saying: 'Make me feel proud of what you do while I am here in heaven.'

So, are Sir Syed's boys and girls making him proud? Well, they don't seem to be doing much to make him happy in heaven. Before the second wave of the COVID-19 pandemic considerably curtailed travel, this writer spent one week at Aligarh in February 2021. Accompanied by Dr Rahat Abrar, former public relations officer at the university, I visited some of the old buildings and institutions created during Sir Syed's lifetime. Not many students were on campus or in their hostel rooms as classes were being held online as per COVID-19 protocol. The scene was not a very happy one. Whatever small fraction of students we saw or even met, they didn't inspire much confidence. Missing was the zeitgeist once so characteristic of the Aligarh boys. Aligarh, we have seen in a previous chapter, was not established just to hand out degrees. Its purpose was not just to create an army of employable youths. It was created to give leadership to the community and the country. And leadership here doesn't mean political leadership alone. Iqbal had described the kind of leadership he expected from Muslim youth in a beautiful couplet:

Sabaq phir padh sadaqat ka adalat ka shujaat ka
Liya jayega tujhse kaam duniya ki imamat ka

(Read again the lessons of truth, justice and bravery
You will be called upon to lead the world).

So, when Iqbal talks of imamat or leadership, he doesn't merely mean the leadership that imams provide during prayers at mosques. He is talking about leadership on the global stage, which Muslim youths must provide. Since Iqbal had a special bond with AMU, he wanted its students to excel in different fields of human knowledge. Iqbal was only articulating through his couplet what Sir Syed strove for all his life.

The mission of Sir Syed was to infuse a new spirit in them to realize their potential as the best educationists and scientists, to work hard to reclaim the lost glory and regain their self-respect and to regain the lost paradise, not by guile and deceit, but by the light of knowledge, awareness, and enlightenment. He knew that Western education had accumulated and created a reservoir of scientific knowledge and that instead of obscurantism and useless tautology, the way forward was only through the light the chain of humanity had, for the time being, handed to the west and its educational institutions and system. Sir Syed's call to attain Western education was unequivocal, and he stood his ground despite strong opposition from many in his community.[2]

Sir Syed succeeded in his mission despite strong opposition from many in his community because of his large-hearted tolerance, resilience and commitment to achieve his goals. As inheritors of Sir Syed's legacy, students of Aligarh Muslim University, in the midst of the centennial celebrations at varsity, would do well to reclaim the dream of their founder and of many of his associates, like Mohsinul Mulk, Viqarul Mulk, Zainul Abideen, Shibli Nomani, Altaf Hussain Hali, Maulana Chiragh Ali, Maulana Zakaullah and Deputy Nazir Ahmed.

Why is Aligarh different from other universities in the world? It is different not just because it has some of India's architecturally marvellous buildings or because it has around 30,000 students. It is different because of the unique culture and ethos it inculcates among its students. Let us understand it with an anecdote. Athar Parvez joined AMU in 1941 and spent over a decade there before he became an established Urdu writer, authoring several books, including many for children. In 1977, when AMU was celebrating the centennial of MAO College (founded in 1877), Parvez came out with a delightful book, *Aligarh se Aligarh Tak* (From Aligarh to Aligarh), a fascinating account of life and times on the campus. Though he centred his narration on Shamshad Market, the bustling bazaar adjacent to the AMU campus, his book carries interesting stories he had heard from the people he befriended and met in Aligarh.

Parvez calls Shamshad Market the 'pulse' of Aligarh. When he says Aligarh, he doesn't mean the city, 166 km from Delhi by road, but Aligarh Muslim University. He says that if you want to understand the Muslim mind in India, don't go anywhere else. Come to AMU and spend some days at Shamshad Market. With its shops for stationery, books and shoes, and its barbers, sherwani-making tailors and tea stalls sitting chock-a-block there, Shamshad is like any other market in mofussil India. Yet, there is something unique about it. It is perhaps the only place abutting a university where so many educated people, or those pretending to being educated, spend countless hours at ramshackle tea houses. Accompanied by snacks like crunchy namakpada and sweets like barfi often served at tables amidst swarms of flies in the day and mosquitos in the evening, the sugary tea served here is sipped over endless conversation. The conversations here feature everything from Imran Khan to Joe Biden, from Modi to the model and television personality Malaika Arora. This is the adda for wannabe poets and fledgling writers too. They read out and recite their passionate poems and stories and receive applause of *'wah, wah'* from friends.

Amidst all this, one thing is conspicuous by its absence. It is silence. Everyone here talks loudly, whether it is to call the waiters or their friends zipping around on bikes. Parvez also recalls the days when a bicycle-stand owner rented out bicycles for a few anaas per hour. Since it was so cheap to rent, the boys would deposit their identity cards with the stand owner and rent bicycles when they needed to go to the city. Or to meet apas (sisters, but the term apa was used also as a cover for girlfriend) at the Abdullah Girls' College, a no-zone for boys unless the meeting was for 'genuine' reasons. The boys rented bicycles also to go to the movies beyond the kathpula, inside the city. The old movie theatre Tasveer Mahal, a few minutes' walk from Sir Syed Hall (South) at the quadrangle, attracted only those who loved Dilip Kumar, Madhubala, Dev Anand, Nargis, Raj Kapoor, Vyjayanthimala and their ilk and had patience for old Hindi films of the golden era. New releases were always displayed at the more modern-looking cinema halls in the city, like Apsara and Novelty. Now, many multiplexes have come up, and even Tasveer Mahal, an institution in itself, is metamorphosing into one.

Since Parvez is a good storyteller, he keeps readers rivetted with his tales about or from people he met on the campus. There is one story Parvez says he heard from Dr Zakir Hussain, who piloted AMU through some of the toughest years (1948–1956). Pervez quotes Zakir Sahab:

Once an American millionaire reached Oxford and appreciated a lawn he saw. He was enchanted by it. As if someone had prodded him, the American millionaire asked, 'How much does it cost to create such a lawn?' The professor accompanying the millionaire said he headed the humanities department and didn't know the details about that. 'If you want, I can summon the gardener and ask him.' 'Call him,' the millionaire said. 'I want exactly this kind of lawn back home, how much will it cost,' asked the millionaire. The gardener replied, 'Sir, it doesn't cost much. A few dollars, just a few dollars. I believe you have the land. Just pave it a little and plant the grass in it. When the grass grows a little, run a roller on it. And keep doing that for around five-hundred years. You will get a similar lawn.'[3]

Moral of the story: nothing comes easily. Just as Rome was not built in a day, a seat of learning like AMU didn't come up in one night. No magic wand was used to turn around things; no Aladdin's lamp worked wonders here. The struggle was long, energy-sapping. The old Sir Syed worked tirelessly, facing stiff resistance, inviting the wrath of the conservatives, including a fury of fatwas from maulvis—not just from India but from Mecca too. A beautiful Urdu couplet encapsulates the trials and tribulations that went into creating a seat of learning like AMU:

'*Seencha hai isko khoon se hum tishna labon ne*
Tab jake is andaz ka maikhana bana hai

(We the thirsty have reared it with blood
And then this tavern was created).'

As AMU celebrates its centennial, its students should think of the challenges the varsity faces. The Corona-pandemic-induced lockdown prevented the AMU authorities from celebrating the occasion with pomp and show, though some of the historic buildings on the campus were lit with decorative lights. Prime Minister Narendra Modi addressed the university community, the worldwide alumni and other well-wishers via video conference. In that historic speech, Modi's first to AMU, the prime minister called AMU a 'mini-India'. He said:

> People tell me that the AMU campus is like a city in itself. We see a mini-India among different departments, dozens of hostels, thousands of teachers and professors. The diversity which we see here is not only the strength of this university, but also of entire nation.[4]

The 'mini-India', this microcosm of India ... its pluralistic character was created and first demonstrated by the founder himself. He led from the front to hail India as a country for all. Many instances of his efforts to promote communal harmony have been cited in previous chapters. Sir Syed showed that he was secular in his actions too. He had many Hindu friends,

> 'including Raja Jaikisan Das, whom he invited to the rasme bismillah of his grandson Ross Masood. Addressing the guests, Sir Syed remarked: "My clean-shaven friend (Das) is here and my grandson is sitting beside him. He is my friend and brother. Syed Mahmood (Sir Syed's son) calls him uncle while he is 'dada Raja' to my grandson Ross Masood".'

Mohan Bhagwat of the RSS would have also found that much before the cow vigilantes began using violence against people in the name of cow protection, Sir Syed had opposed the slaughter of cows and counselled Muslims to respect the sentiments of Hindus and slaughter only goat and sheep on Bakri Eid. He would have also noticed that 'AMU has kept its doors open for everyone since its inception and that its first graduate was a Hindu'—Ishwari Prasad.[5]

Students of AMU today have to show the same tolerance and large-heartedness that Sir Syed demonstrated. And they have, time and again. A section of the media has shown its bias on a number of occasions in reporting incidents at AMU. Ever since Twitter came into our lives, many have taken to the micro-blogging site to paint AMU in bad colours. On 29 May 2017, a debate on Twitter began over whether non-Muslim students at AMU were forced to fast for Ramzan. It began when an advocate at the Delhi High Court, Prashant Patel, wrote on Twitter:

> In Aligarh muslim university hostels, Lunch, Breakfast is not being served to Hindu students due to #Ramadan https://t.co/ghUntAGj2p
> — Prashant Patel Umrao (@ippatel) May 29, 2017[6]

A storm on Twitter began, with many attacking AMU while others called the post fake. On investigating the matter, by checking with both the AMU spokesperson and Hindu students on the campus, The Quint found it to be false:

> **The Quint** also reached out to Jyoti Bhaskar, a mass communication student at AMU, who said, 'It is a sad thing to bring a religious angle into the story.

'In February, when I was fasting during Navratri, the mess used to provide milk and bananas. We should respect the religious sentiments,' Bhaskar added.

He said that in MM hall, where he lives, breakfast and dinner is provided as usual. However, lunch is not provided because most of the people working in the mess are fasting, and it is difficult for them to keep fast and work at the same time. He himself goes to canteens around the campus for his lunch.

However, he added that the non-fasting students who couldn't afford to eat out can still get lunch if they write an application to the Senior Food Monitor to provide them food, and the authorities will do the needful.[7]

This is just one example of how baseless, malicious campaigns seek to tarnish the image of AMU. The AMU community, especially the students, will have to be prepared to counter such vilification campaigns. Apart from showing restraint while protesting the injustices done to them or to the larger Muslim community or to anyone else in the country, they must remain non-violent. There was a time when students and teachers at AMU would write articles and letters to the editor in the national dailies, highlighting incidents of slight, bias or violence against minorities. Now, except for a few, this writer doesn't see many names from AMU making reasoned arguments for the rights of minorities in the national press. Why is it so? It is so because of the general downfall in standards in the academic and non-academic arena at the university. Essay competitions and debates were part of life on the campus. These cultural events moulded the students and made them confident.

Doha-based Dr Nadeem Zafar Jilani had joined AMU in 1986 in the twelfth standard, taking the science stream, and went on to do his MBBS and MD (paediatrics) from AMU. 'The cultural scene on the campus in the 1980s and 1990s was very vibrant. Each hall of residence would hold its cultural weeks, evocatively named "Ibtida 86", "Aghaz 90", "Ehsaas 91" or "Masood 88", recalls Jilani. The most popular among the cultural weeks, recalls Jilani, were those organized by the Abdullah Girls' College and Sarojini Naidu Hall, another hall of residence for women students. Though he participated in many other competitions, Bait Bazi is what Jilani really excelled at. Like Antakshari in Hindi, Bait Bazi is a verbal game and a genre of Urdu poetry played by composing Urdu verses. 'For the final prize distribution, winners were invited to the annual hall function of the respective halls of residence. To be invited to the Abdullah Girls' College annual hall function and dinner was a big achievement for male students on the campus. You would wear your best dress or even borrow a suit from a friend to look smartly dressed. Accepting awards there was no less satisfying than winning a Grammy or Oscar as hundreds of girls cheered', recalls Jilani, who is also an established Urdu poet.

Yes, in the last one year or so, the Coronavirus-induced lockdown has disrupted activities at the campus, and even the students' union elections have not been held for the last two years.

We have discussed how the union elections produced good student leaders, many of whom went on to play notable roles in national politics. A few years ago, during the controversy over Pakistan founder Mohammad Ali Jinnah's portrait at AMU campus, this writer was appalled to see a student leader getting mauled in a debate by a mediocre media person at a news channel. Where have student leaders like Arif Mohammed Khan, Azam Khan, Javed Habib, Akhtarul Wasey, Mohammed Aeeb, Mufti Mohsin Athar, Ishtiaq Abdi, Bashir Ahmed Khan, Moonis Raza, Ali Ashraf Fatmi, Qamar Alam, Irfanullah, Qaisar Mohammed and Dr Ali Ameer gone? Trained at the students' union debates, they became forceful speakers who spoke and argued convincingly.

Former students' union president and Rajya Sabha member Mohammed Adeeb recalls a meeting in Delhi a couple of years ago where the late Javed Habib publicly admitted that leaders like Adeeb were products of an era when student leaders interacted with senior community leaders to understand the pulse of the community. Recalls Adeeb: 'Javed Habib said that he could write and speak better than Adeeb but still considered Adeeb a bigger leader because the latter had got sohbat, or company of some of the leading Muslim leaders of post-Independence India.' So the likes of Adeeb were groomed in the company of eminent religious and political leaders and educationists like Maulana Ali Miyan Nadvi, Ishtiaq Qureshi, Dr Faridi, Shafiqur Rahman, Zafar Ahmed Siddiqui, Saiyid Hamid, Ali M Khusro and Monis Raza. When Jawaharlal Nehru University (JNU) student leader Kanhaiya Kumar hit the headlines in February 2016 after he was arrested on a sedition charge for allegedly raising anti-national slogans at a protest meet on the campus, Adeeb raised a toast to him: 'I was happy that a young student leader had emerged on the national scene but I wondered why AMU had not produced its own Kanhaiya Kumar.'

Ishtiaq Ali, a student leader at AMU in the 1980s, says that till the mid–1980s many bright students joined student politics. 'Many of them were good at studies as well as at student politics. Then many bad elements intruded and spoiled the atmosphere,' says Ishtiaq Ali. Tariq Hasan, in his book *The Aligarh Movement and the Making of the Indian Muslim Mind 1857-2002,* holds the movement for the minority character of AMU responsible for creation of the culture of mass protests and violence. Finally, in 1981, Indira Gandhi accorded minority character to AMU, ending a long struggle. Writes Hasan:

> A turbulent phase at AMU had ended after nearly fifteen years but the damage had been done. The culture of mass protest and violence had taken root at AMU and an institution which used to pride itself on its discipline had fallen prey to the designs of different political parties and all of whom viewed AMU merely as a shortcut to the Muslim vote bank.[8]

In recent times AMU has thrown up student leaders like Fahad Ahmad, Mashkoor Usmani, Faizul Hassan, Salman Ahmad, Syed Sharique Ahmed, Abu Affan Farooqui, Amir Qutub, Huzaifa Aamir and Nabeel Usmani. Fahad Ahmed, a former student leader at AMU and now at Tata Institute of Social Sciences (TISS), Mumbai, where he is currently a senior research fellow, blames the Lyngdoh committee recommendations as one of the reasons for the lack of strong student leaders at universities. In December 2005, the human resource development ministry (now the education ministry) formed a committee headed by former Chief Election Commissioner J.M. Lyngdoh to examine certain aspects of students' body and students' union elections at Indian colleges and universities. 'On 26 May 2006, the Lyngdoh Committee submitted its report.'[9]

'One of the recommendations of the Lyngdoh report is that no candidate can fight elections twice for executive posts in students' union elections. At AMU, the president, vice president and secretary are executive posts. The report says that a candidate cannot contest another election if he or she has won or lost one of these three posts. I think the candidates who lose one of these posts in an election should be given a second chance to contest and try their luck. Most student leaders lose interest in union elections after losing the first election. A student union election is a good training ground for future politicians,' says Fahad Ahmad.

AMU today stands at a crossroads. A sword hangs on its minority character as it awaits the verdict of the Supreme Court in the appeal filed in 2006 to retain the minority character of the university. Though the anti-CAA–NRC issue is on the backburner because of the outbreak of the Coronavirus pandemic, it has not disappeared. Once the Centre begins the process of implementation of CAA, students at AMU may not sit quiet about the police brutality at the university on 15 December 2019 which left many students severely injured.[10]

The role of students is critical in the making or unmaking of a university. AMU, being the intellectual hub of Indian Muslims, has a big responsibility to mould the mizaj or temperament of its student community. The teacher-student relationship at the university has to be strengthened. Since it is basically a residential university, residential life here has to be made healthier.

AMU has to be preserved and protected for the coming generations.

Acknowledgements

THE idea of a book was at the back of my mind for long. But it needed prodding, a trigger. My daughters—Nayab, Sara, Zareen—provided that trigger by asking me one day: 'Daddy, when will you become an author?' The question unsettled me. It set me thinking, as I was to turn fifty in January 2021.

The Aligarh Muslim University, my alma mater, had also announced celebrations as it turned 100 in December 2020. Though the pandemic has kept the celebrations muted, the significance of AMU turning 100 cannot be overemphasized. So, my first book had to be about AMU and Indian Muslims.

I took my children's question as a challenge and began searching for its answer. Isn't the trite proverb 'where there is a will there is a way' true? Once I resolved I had to write a book and the book had to be about AMU, the seemingly herculean task became easy. Doors opened and help poured in from many corners. A big thank you to my beautiful daughters for being the initiators of this project.

If my daughters ignited a dormant dream, their mother became a perpetual pillar of strength. Her constant push, reminders that I had to finish a book and continuous encouragement kept me focused to the goal that I had set myself. Since writing is a lonely profession, there were countless hours when I secluded myself in the corner of my house, my fingers dancing on the keyboard. My gratitude to my wife Heena for all the love and patience she showed. Her sister Zeenat too helped in many ways. Thanks to her as well.

A number of people at AMU helped me with valuable suggestions and guidance about the books I needed to read before I wrote on the university. They include former PRO and Director of Urdu Academy Dr Rahat Abrar, whom I reached out to several times. He was also kind enough to give me a guided tour of the heritage section of the university in February 2001. Professor of Mass Communications Shafey Kidwai opened his heart and the doors of his beautiful house. He sent me a list of some important books to read. I am grateful to him for his warm hospitality and important advice. Deputy Director of Sir Syed Academy Dr Mohammed Shahid was a big support and took pains to send me many important publications from the academy, including early biographies of Sir Syed and MAO College. I am indebted to many other teachers and students too, whom I spoke to while writing this book.

I am also grateful to my siblings, especially younger brother Dr Md Qutbuddin for his scholarly advice and constant encouragement. He too lent me some important books. The silent love and admiration of other siblings, Qamar Alam,

Ashrafuddin and younger sister Zakira, and many cousins cannot be repaid. I remain indebted to them all.

My gratitude is also to good friend and former colleague Sameer Arshad Khatlani who connected me to Swati Chopra at HarperCollins India. Swati, with her constant encouragement and valuable suggestions, made the task of writing this book easier. She was magnanimous in giving me enough time to reflect and write. A big thank you to her.

General Secretary of Anjuman Taraqqi Urdu (Hind) and my good friend Athar Farooqui sent me Ross Masood's only complete biography (in Urdu) by Hakim Syed Zillur Rahman. This book immensely helped me write the chapter on Ross Masood. A big thank you to Athar Sahab.

Since the book was written during the Coronavirus-induced lockdown, I remained glued to the computer screen for hours and needed doses of caffeine to keep me awake. Saba kept supplying endless cups of coffee while I spent hours at my writing desk. A big thank you to her too.

At *The Times of India*, I have enjoyed complete freedom to think, reflect and write. The paper has helped me get a better perspective on life and people. A huge thank you to TOI and my many colleagues.

Notes

Introduction

1   Salman Khurshid, *Visible Muslim, Invisible Citizen*, (Rupa Publications India Pvt. Ltd, 2019), p. 80.

2   'PM Modi calls AMU "mini-India", says politics can wait but development can't', *Indian Express*, 22 December 2020. https://indianexpress.com/article/india/aligarh-muslim-university-centenary-celebration-pm-modi-7114450/

3   David Lelyveld, *Aligarh's First Generation: Muslim Solidarity in British India*, (Oxford University Press, 1996), p. 31.

4   Tufail Ahmad, 'Question Islamism of iconic poet', *The New Indian Express*, 9 November 2013. https://www.newindianexpress.com/opinions/2013/nov/09/Question-Islamism-of-iconic-poet-535321.html

5   Dr Rafiq Zakaria, *Iqbal, Shair aur Siyasatdan*, translated by Prof. Abdus Sattar Dalvi, (Anjuman Taraqqi Urdu (Hind), 1995), p. 137.

6 Juhi Gupta and Abdur Raheem Kidwai, *Oxford of the East: Aligarh Muslim University (1920–2020)*, Centenary Commemorative Volume, (Viva Books Pvt. Ltd, 2021), p. 294.

7 M Hashim Kidwai, *The Life and Times of a Nationalist Muslim*, (Universal Book House, 2015), p. 142.

8 Rajmohan Gandhi, *Understanding the Muslim Mind*, (Penguin Random House India, 2000), p. 87.

9 Ibid., p. 120.

10 'Profile of Hasrat Mohani', Rekhta. https://www.rekhta.org/poets/hasrat-mohani/profile.

11 Ibid.

12 Juhi Gupta and Abdur Raheem Kidwai, *Oxford of the East: Aligarh Muslim University (1920–2020)*, Centenary Commemorative Volume, (Viva Books Pvt. Ltd, 2021), p. 56.

13 Ibid., p. 57.

14 M. Mujeeb, *Dr Zakir Hussain*, (National Book Trust, 1991), p. 26

1 The Making of AMU

1 PRO, AMU, 26 Jan 2020.

2 G.I.F. Graham, *The Life and Work of Syed Ahmed Khan*, (Sir Syed Academy, 1974), p. 163.

3 Ibid., p. 246.

4 Ibid., p. 153.

5 Ibid., p. 153.

6 Ibid., p. 161.

7 A new order of knighthood the British Crown created in recognition of services to the British empire.

8 Khushwant Singh, 'Book review: Rafiq Zakaria's "Muhammad and The Quran"', India Today, 25 June 2013. https://www.indiatoday.in/magazine/society-the-arts/story/19920131-book-review-rafiq-zakarias-muhammad-and-the-quran-765770-2013-06-25

9 Rajmohan Gandhi, *Understanding the Muslim Mind*, (Penguin Books, 1986, 2000), p. 30.

10 Altaf Husain Hali, *Hayat-i-Javed*, (National Council for Promotion of Urdu, 2004), p. 165.

11 Rasheed Ahmed Siddiqui, *Ashufta Bayani Meri*, (Maktaba Jamia Ltd, 2012), p. 139.

12 From an interview with the author on 7 February 2021 at Aligarh. Used with permission.

13 Juhi Gupta and Abdur Raheem Kidwai, *Oxford of the East: Aligarh Muslim University (1920–2020)*, Centenary Commemorative Volume, (Viva Books Pvt. Ltd, 2021), p. 132.

14 S.K. Bhatnagar, *History of the MAO College*, (Sir Syed Academy, AMU, 2019), p. 36

15 G.F.I. Graham, *The Life and Work of Syed Ahmed Khan*, (Sir Syed Academy, AMU, 2019), p. 145.

16 David Lelyveld, *Aligarh's First Generation*, (Oxford University Press, 1996), p. 154.

17 Ibid., p. 152.

18 'The Mohammedan Anglo-Oriental College Aligarh and its Supporters', Sir Syed, Aligarh Institute Gazette, 15 December 1885.

19 S.K. Bhatnagar, *History of the MAO College*, (Sir Syed Academy, AMU, 2019), p. 48.

20 Rajmohan Gandhi, *Understanding the Muslim Mind*, (Penguin Books India, 2000), p. 40.

21 S.K. Bhatnagar, *History of the MAO College*, (Sir Syed Academy, AMU, 2019), p. 88.

22 Iftikhar Alam Khan, *Sir Syed: Daroone Khana*, (Aligarh, Educational Book House, 2020), p. 295.

23 S.K. Bhatnagar, *History of the MAO College*, (Sir Syed Academy, AMU, 2019), p. 93.

24 Juhi Gupta and Abdur Raheem Kidwai, *Oxford of the East: Aligarh Muslim University (1920–2020)*, Centenary Commemorative Volume, (Viva Books Pvt Ltd, 2021), p. 147.

25 Ibid., p. 152.

26 Ibid.

27 Ibid.

28 Rajmohan Gandhi, *Understanding the Muslim Mind*, (Penguin Books India, 2000), p. 88.

29 Juhi Gupta and Abdur Raheem Kidwai, *Oxford of the East: Aligarh Muslim University (1920–2020)*, Centenary Commemorative Volume, (Viva Books Pvt. Ltd, 2021), p. 157.

30 Ibid., p. 158.
31 Ibid., p. 159.
32 Ibid., p. 62.
33 Ibid., p. 169.
34 Ibid., p. 162.
35 Ibid., p. 176.
36 Naseem Ansari, *Jawabe Dost*, (Lucknow, Nizami Press Book Depo), p. 175.

2 Aligarh and Partition Pangs

1   Mukhtar Masood, *Awaz-e-Dost*, (New Delhi, M.R. Publications, 2018), p. 240.
2   Rafiq Zakaria, *The Man Who Divided India*, (Popular Prakashan Pvt Ltd, 2001), p. 165.
3   Ibid., p. 165
4   'BJP MP Sees Red Over Jinnah Portrait in Aligarh Muslim University, Writes to V-C', News18.com, 1 May 2018. https://www.news18.com/news/india/bjp-mp-sees-red-over-jinnah-portrait-in-aligarh-muslim-university-writes-to-v-c-1734557.html
5   From an interview with the author on 4 March 2021 on phone. Used with permission.
6   M Hamid Ansari, *By Many a Happy Accident: Recollections of a Life*, (Rupa Publications India Pvt. Ltd 2021), p. 322.
7   Rajmohan Gandhi, *Understanding the Muslim Mind*, (Penguin Random House India Pvt Ltd, 2000), p. 145.
8   Ibid., p. 145.
9   Tariq Hasan, *The Aligarh Movement and the Making of the Indian Muslim Mind (1857–2002)*, (Rupa Publications India Pvt. Ltd, 2005), p. 222.
10 Rafiq Zakaria, *The Man Who Divided India*, (Popular Prakashan Pvt Ltd, 2001), p. 73.
11 Ibid., p. 71.
12 Ibid., p. 75.
13 Rajmohan Gandhi, *Understanding the Muslim Mind*, (Penguin Random House India Pvt Ltd, 2000), p. 150.

14   Tariq Hasan, *The Aligarh Movement and the Making of the Indian Muslim Mind (1857–2002)*, (Rupa Publications India Pvt. Ltd, 2005), p. 224.

15   Rafiq Zakaria, *The Man Who Divided India*, (Popular Prakashan Pvt Ltd, 2001), p. 82.

16   Ibid., p. 83.

17   Ibid., p. 84.

18   Tariq Hasan, *The Aligarh Movement and the Making of the Indian Muslim Mind (1857-2002)*, (Rupa Publications India Pvt. Ltd, 2005) p. 240.

19   Ibid., p. 241.

3 The Inheritor of Sir Syed's Legacy

1   Juhi Gupta and Abdur Raheem Kidwai, *Oxford of the East: Aligarh Muslim University (1920–2020)*, Centenary Commemorative Volume, (Viva Books Pvt Ltd, 2021), p. 98.

2   Hakim Syed Zillur Rahman, *Ross Masood*, (Anjuman Taraqqi Urdu [India], 2018), p. 30.

3   Ibid., p. 31.

4   Ibid., p. 59.

5   British Residency, Hyderabad, Wikipedia. https://en.wikipedia.org/wiki/British_Residency,_Hyderabad

6   Hakim Syed Zillur Rahman, *Ross Masood*, (Anjuman Taraqqi Urdu [India], 2018), p. 60.

7   Ibid., Page 104.

8   Akbar Ahmed, *Journey into Europe: Islam, Immigration and Identity*, (Brookings Institution Press, 2018), p. 105.

9   Ibid., p. 106.

10   Ibid., p. 122.

11   Hakim Syed Zillur Rahman, *Ross Masood*, (Anjuman Taraqqi Urdu [India], 2018), p.107.

12   Hakim Syed Zillur Rahman, *Ross Masood*, (Anjuman Taraqqi Urdu [India], 2018), p. 47.

13   Ibid., p. 116.

14   Ibid., p. 117.

15 Juhi Gupta and Abdur Raheem Kidwai, *Oxford of the East: Aligarh Muslim University (1920–2020)*, Centenary Commemorative Volume, (Viva Books Pvt. Ltd, 2021), p. 91

16 Juhi Gupta and Abdur Raheem Kidwai, *Oxford of the East: Aligarh Muslim University (1920–2020)*, Centenary Commemorative Volume, (Viva Books Pvt Ltd, 2021), p. 92.

17 Hakim Syed Zillur Rahman, *Ross Masood*, (Anjuman Taraqqi Urdu [India], 2018), p. 123.

18 Ibid., p. 123.

19 Ibid., p. 123.

20 Ibid., p. 126.

21 Ibid., p. 147.

22 Ibid., p.175.

23 Ibid., p. 178

4 After the Storm: Two Stalwarts Who Saved AMU

1   Mohammed Wajihuddin, 'When Maulana Azad played sitar at the Taj', The Times of India, 21 March 2020.

2   Mukhtar Masood, *Awaz-e-Dost*, (New Delhi, M.R. Publications, 2018), p. 231.

3   Dr Rahat Abrar, *Muslim Taaleeem-e-Niswan ke Sau Saal: Chilman se Chand Tak,* (Educational Publishing House, 2011), p. 12.

4   'Poems by Akbar Ilahabadi' tr. Miriam Murtuza. http://www.columbia.edu/itc/mealac/pritchett/00urduhindilinks/txt_akbarallahabadi_miriammurtuza.pdf

5   M. Mujeeb, *Dr Zakir Hussain*, (National Book Trust, India, 1991), p. 173.

6   Tariq Hasan, *The Aligarh Movement*, (Rupa Publications India Pvt Ltd, 2006), p. 252.

7   M. Mujeeb, *Dr Zakir Hussain*, (National Book Trust, India, 1991), p. 161.

8   Ibid., p. 160.

9   Juhi Gupta and Abdur Raheem Kidwai, *Oxford of the East: Aligarh Muslim University (1920–2020)*, Centenary Commemorative Volume, (Viva Books Pvt Ltd, 2021), p. 62.

10 Dr Abidullah Ansari Ghazi, *Jahad-e-Musalsal: Aligarh Se Aligarh Tak*, (Chicago, Iqra International Educational Foundation, 2017), p. 234

11 Tariq Hasan, *The Aligarh Movement*, (Rupa Publications India Pvt Ltd, 2006), p. 250.

12 Juhi Gupta and Abdur Raheem Kidwai, *Oxford of the East: Aligarh Muslim University (1920–2020)*, Centenary Commemorative Volume, (Viva Books Pvt Ltd, 2021), p. 61.

13 S.K. Bhatnagar, *History of the MAO College, Aligarh*, (Aligarh, Sir Syed Academy, 2019), p. 110.

14 Mayank Austen Soofi, 'Delhi Speeches—Abul Kalam Azad, Jama Masjid, 1947', The Delhi Walla, 12 November 2015. http://thedelhiwalla.blogspot.com/2015/11/delhi-speeches-abul-kalam-azad-jama.html

15 Priyanka Dasgupta, 'Maulana Azad's family donates historical treasure trove to AMU', *The Times of India*, 7 May 2017. http://timesofindia.indiatimes.com/articleshow/58564634.cms?utm_source=contentofinterest&utm_medium=text&utm_campaign=cppst

16 Rajmohan Gandhi, *Understanding the Muslim Mind*, (Penguin Random House India, 2000), p. 303.

5 A Modern Institution or Madrassa?

1 Juhi Gupta and Abdur Raheem Kidwai, *Oxford of the East: Aligarh Muslim University (1920–2020)*, Centenary Commemorative Volume, (Viva Books Pvt Ltd, 2021), p. 64.

2 From an interview with the author on 8 April 2021 on phone. Used with permission.

3 Sunil Sethi, 'AMU students resort to violence over professor's 'criminals in campus' remarks', *India Today*, 26 November 2013. https://www.indiatoday.in/magazine/special-report/story/19810228-aligarh-muslim-university-students-resort-to-violence-over-professors-criminals-in-campus-remarks-772704-2013-11-26

4 Ibid.

5   Najma Mahmood, *Saiyid Hamid: Ke Gum Us Mein Hain Afaaq*, (Vision Publications, 2003), p. 361.

6   Lt Gen. Zameer Uddin Shah, *The Sarkari Mussalman: Life and Travails of a Soldier Educationist*, (Konark Publishers Private Ltd, 2018), p. 152.

7   Tariq Hasan, *The Aligarh Movement and the Making of the Indian Muslim Mind (1857-2002)*, (Rupa Publications India Pvt Ltd, 2006), p. 255.

8   From an interview with the author conducted at Adeeb's House in Delhi on 9 February 2021. Used with permission.

9   Anil Maheshwari, *Aligarh Muslim University: Perfect Past and Precarious Present*, (UBS Publishers' Distributors Ltd, 2001), p. 33.

10   Ibid., p. 47.

11   Ibid., p. 48.

12   Ibid., p. 56

13   From an interview with the author conducted at Wasey's House in Delhi on 9 February 2021. Used with permission.

14   Tariq Hasan, *The Aligarh Movement and the Making of the Indian Muslim Mind (1857-2002)*, (Rupa Publications India Pvt. Ltd, 2006), p. 257

15   Anil Maheshwari, *Aligarh Muslim University: Perfect Past and Precarious Present*, (UBS Publishers' Distributors Ltd, 2001), p. 52.

16   Ibid., p. 53.

17   Ibid., p. 59.

18   Juhi Gupta and Abdur Raheem Kidwai, *Oxford of the East: Aligarh Muslim University (1920–2020)*, Centenary Commemorative Volume, (Viva Books Pvt Ltd, 2021), p. 64.

19   Ibid., p. 64.

20   Ibid., p. 69.

6 Glorious Past, Precarious Present

1   The author had attended this meet and noted the statement Khan made. Used with Khan's permission.

2   Sir Hamilton Gibb, *Mohammedanism*, (Oxford University Press, 1957), p. 181.

3   Frank F. Islam, 'Frank Islam of US gives back $2 mn to alma mater Aligarh Muslim University – The Economic Times', 13 April 2015. https://frankislam.com/article/frank-islam-of-us-gives-back-2m-to-alma-mater-aligarh-muslim-university/

4   'Entrepreneurs are made, not born: Frank Islam, Indian-American entrepreneur', *The Economic Times*, 21 June 2015. https://economictimes.indiatimes.com/opinion/interviews/entrepreneurs-are-made-not-born-frank-islam-indian-american-entrepreneur/articleshow/47755071.cms?utm_source=contentofinterest&utm_medium=text&utm_campaign=cppst

5   Mohd Faisal Fareed, 'Windfall for AMU: gets Rs 70 lakh from alumni, jewellery for museum on Founder's Day', *Indian Express*, 22 October 2015 https://indianexpress.com/article/cities/lucknow/windfall-for-amu-gets-rs-70-lakh-from-alumni-jewellery-for-museum-on-founders-day/

6   From an interview with the author conducted in Mumbai on 15 April 2021. Used with permission.

7   Zia Us Salam and Uzma Ausaf, *Shaheen Bagh: From a Protest to a Movement*, (Bloomsbury Publishing India Pvt Ltd, 2020), p. 14.

8   Karwan e Mohabbat, 'The Siege of Aligarh Muslim University: A Fact Finding Report', News Click, 24 December 2019. https://www.newsclick.in/Siege-Aligarh-Muslim-University-Fact-Finding-Report

9   Ibid.

10 Ibid.

11 'A Timeline: The Cases Against Dr Kafeel Khan and His Arrests', The Wire, 2 September 2020. https://thewire.in/rights/kafeel-khan-arrest-cases-timeline

12 Ibid.

13 Ibid.

14 Ibid.

15 Ibid.

16 ANI, 'f Uddhav Thackeray goes to Ayodhya, I also will go there to construct Babri Masjid: Farhan Azmi', *The New Indian Express*, 30 January 2020. https://www.newindianexpress.com/nation/2020/

jan/30/if-uddhav-thackeray-goes-to-ayodhya-i-also-will-go-there-to-construct-babri-masjid-farhan-azmi-2096605.html
17 Ibid.
18 Manoj Singh, 'A Single Photograph Was All it Took to Dramatically Alter Dr Kafeel Khan's Life', The Wire, 3 September 2020. https://thewire.in/rights/dr-kafeel-khan-release-gorakhpur-brd-medical-arrest
19 Ibid.
20 '"More Brutal Than Even Jamia": AMU Fact Finding Report Accuses UP Police of Violence, Islamophobia', The Wire, 24 December 2019. https://thewire.in/government/amu-caa-protests-up-police
21 Juhi Gupta and Abdur Raheem Kidwai, *Oxford of the East: Aligarh Muslim University (1920–2020)*, Centenary Commemorative Volume, (Viva Books Pvt. Ltd, 2021), p. 329.
22 PTI, 'Sudarshan TV Seeks Live Telecast Of SC Hearing Against The UPSC Jihad Programme', *Outlook*, 17 September 2020. https://www.outlookindia.com/website/story/india-news-sudarshan-tv-case-centre-tells-sc-to-regulate-digital-media-first/360462
23 'I&B Ministry Says "UPSC Jihad" Show Was "Offensive", Allows Airing With "Modifications"', The Wire, 19 November 2020. https://thewire.in/government/sudarshan-news-upsc-jihad-suresh-chavhanke-ministry-ib-offesnive-communal-attitudes
24 Ibid.
25 Ibid.
26 Tariq Hasan, *The Aligarh Movement and the Making of the Indian Muslim Mind (1857-2002)*, (Rupa Publications India Pvt Ltd, 2006), p. 269.
27 Ibid., p. 270.

7 The Tablighi Footprint

1 From an interview with the author conducted in Mumbai on 15 April 2021. Used with permission.
2 Ziya Us Salam, *Inside the Tablighi Jamaat*, (HarperCollins Publishers India, 2020), p. 35.
3 Ibid., p. 24.

4   'Tablighi Jamaat', Wikipedia, https://en.wikipedia.org/wiki/Tablighi_Jamaat

5   Ziya Us Salam, *Inside the Tablighi Jamaat*, (HarperCollins Publishers India, 2020), p. 27.

6   Ibid., p. 3.

7   Ibid., p. 9.

8   Apoorva Mandhani, 'Possible that cops picked up 36 Tablighi foreigners to "maliciously prosecute" them—court', The Print, 16 December 2020. https://theprint.in/india/possible-that-cops-picked-up-36-tablighi-foreigners-to-maliciously-prosecute-them-court/567682/

9   Soibam Rocky Singh, Hemani Bhandari, 'Tablighi Jamaat: Much ado about one thing', *The Hindu*, 22 March 2021. https://www.thehindu.com/news/cities/Delhi/tablighi-jamaat-much-ado-about-one-thing/article34126409.ece

10 '"Scapegoats": Bombay High court cancels FIR against 29 foreign Tablighi Jamaat members', *Hindustan Times*, 22 August 2020. https://www.hindustantimes.com/india-news/scapegoats-bombay-high-court-cancels-fir-against-29-foreign-jamaat-members/story-ct8wNaoRENyZsu65k0rVCJ.html

11 Ibid.

8 Reviving Sir Syed's Mission, and Death of a Dream

1   Dr Abidullah Ansari Ghazi, *Jahad-e-Musalsal: Aligarh Se Aligarh Tak*, (Chicago, Iqra International Educational Foundation, 2017), p. 9.

2   Ibid., p. 21.

3   Maqbool Ahmed Siraj, nrindians@googlegroups.com, 11 April 2021

4   Dr Abidullah Ansari Ghazi, *Jahad-e-Musalsal: Aligarh Se Aligarh Tak*, (Chicago, Iqra International Educational Foundation, 2017), p. 344.

5   Ibid., p. 347.

6   Ibid., p. 348.

7   Dr Abidullah Ansari Ghazi, *Jahad-e-Musalsal: Aligarh Se Aligarh Tak*, (Chicago, Iqra International Educational Foundation, p. 348.

8   Ibid., p. 234.

9   Ibid.

10   Ibid., p. 244.
11   Ibid., p. 331.
12   Ibid., p. 334.
13   Ibid., p. 311.

9 Bastion of Liberalism or Hotbed of Islamism?

1   Dr Farida Khanum, *Maulana Maududi: Shakhshiyat aur Tahrik*, (Goodword Books, 2008), p. 9.
2   'History and Background', Jamaat-e-Islami Hind. https://jamaateislamihind.org/eng/about-jamaat/history/
3   Noman Badar Falahi, *Hindustani Talba Mein Tahrik-e-Islami Ki Taariikh*, (unpublished thesis) p. 1.
4   Ibid., p. 5.
5   Ibid.
6   Ibid., p. 6.
7   Ibid., p. 3.
8   Ibid., p. 12.
9   Jamaat-e-Islami Hind, Wikipedia, https://en.wikipedia.org/wiki/Jamaat-e-Islami_Hind
10   Dr Abidullah Ansari Ghazi, *Jahad-e-Musalsal: Aligarh Se Aligarh Tak*, (Chicago, Iqra International Educational Foundation, 2017), p. 167
11   Tariq Hasan, *The Aligarh Movement and the Making of the Indian Muslim Mind 1857-2002*, (Rupa Publications India Pvt. Ltd, 2006), p. 263.
12   Noman Badar Falahi, *Hindustani Talba Mein Tahrik-e-Islami Ki Taariikh*, (unpublished thesis) p. 7.
13   Ibid., p. 8
14   This writer was witness to the scene.
15   Ibid., p. 14.
16   Tariq Hasan, *The Aligarh Movement and the Making of the Indian Muslim Mind 1857-2002*, (Rupa Publications India Pvt Ltd, 2006), p. 262.
17   Ibid., p. 19.
18   Ibid., p. 20.

19   Ibid., p. 24.

20   Danish Khan, 'Muslim South Asia Conference', SOAS University
     of London, 28 October 2013. https://www.soas.ac.uk/south-asia-
     institute/musa/events/file89426.pdf

21   Mohammed   Wajihuddin,   'It's   radicalism   that   appeals
     to educated men', *Times of India*, 7 August 2008. http://
     timesofindia.indiatimes.com/articleshow/3335335.cms?utm_
     source=contentofinterest&utm_medium=text&utm_
     campaign=cppst

22   Tariq Hasan, *The Aligarh Movement and the Making of the Indian
     Muslim Mind 1857-2002*, (Rupa Publications India Pvt. Ltd, 2006),
     p. 264.

23   Chandan Haygunde, 'The history behind the ban on SIMI, and why
     the tribunal is reviewing it', *Indian Express*, 19 May 2019. https://
     indianexpress.com/article/india/the-history-behind-the-ban-on-
     simi-and-why-the-tribunal-is-reviewing-it-5735659/

10 To the Students of AMU

1   Juhi Gupta and Abdur Raheem Kidwai, *Oxford of the East: Aligarh
     Muslim University (1920–2020)*, Centenary Commemorative
     Volume, (Viva Books Pvt. Ltd, 2021), p. 295.

2   Ibid., p. 289.

3   Dr Athar Parvez, *Aligarh Se Aligarh Tak*, (Urdu Ghar, 2007), p. 26.

4   'Government committed to development without discrimination:
     Prime Minister Narendra Modi at AMU', *Times of India*,
     22   December   2020.   http://timesofindia.indiatimes.com/
     articleshow/79851786.cms?utm_source=contentofinterest&utm_
     medium=text&utm_campaign=cppst

5   Mohammed Wajihuddin, 'How Sir Syed Ahmed Khan helped bring
     in Indian renaissance', *Times of India*, 13 October 2008. https://
     timesofindia.indiatimes.com/blogs/beyond-the-burqa/how-sir-
     syed-ahmed-khan-helped-bring-in-indian-renaissance/

6   Abhilash Mullick, 'AMU Not Serving Food to Hindus During
     Ramzan? Here's the Truth', The Quint, 12 June 2017. https://
     www.thequint.com/news/india/amu-not-serving-food-to-hindu-
     during-ramzan-truth#read-more

7   Ibid.
8   Tariq Hasan, *The Aligarh Movement and the Making of the Indian Muslim Mind 1857-2002,* (Rupa Publications India Pvt. Ltd, 2006), p. 258.
9   Lyngdoh Committee Recommendations. https://www.ugc.ac.in/oldpdf/students_pdf/lyngdoh_committeemhrd2712.pdf
10   Ayush Tiwari, 'Beaten, bruised, pelted with stun grenades: Aligarh students recall a night of horror', Newslaundry, 18 December 2019. https://www.newslaundry.com/2019/12/18/december-15-aligarh-muslim-university-students-police-violence

Index

About the Author

Mohammed Wajihuddin is a senior assistant editor with *The Times of India*, Mumbai. Earlier, he worked with *The Indian Express* and the *Asian Age*. A passionate lover of Urdu poetry, he is also a blogger and writes prolifically on issues that are of interest to Indian Muslims. He lives in Mumbai.